STRENGTH *in* STILLNESS

STRENGTH *in* STILLNESS

The POWER *of* TRANSCENDENTAL MEDITATION

BOB ROTH

WITH KEVIN CARR O'LEARY

**SIMON &
SCHUSTER**

London · New York · Sydney · Toronto · New Delhi

A CBS COMPANY

First published in Great Britain by Simon & Schuster UK Ltd, 2018
A CBS COMPANY

1 3 5 7 9 10 8 6 4 2

Simon & Schuster UK Ltd
1st Floor
222 Gray's Inn Road
London WC1X 8HB

www.simonandschuster.co.uk
www.simonandschuster.com.au
www.simonandschuster.co.in

Simon & Schuster Australia, Sydney
Simon & Schuster India, New Delhi

The author and publishers have made all reasonable efforts to contact copyright-
holders for permission, and apologise for any omissions or errors in the
form of credits given. Corrections may be made to future printings.

A CIP catalogue record for this book
is available from the British Library

Hardback ISBN: 978-1-4711-6163-6
eBook ISBN: 978-1-4711-6164-3

Interior design by Carly Loman
Printed and bound by CPI Group (UK) Ltd, Croydon, CR0 4YY

Simon & Schuster UK Ltd are committed to sourcing paper
that is made from wood grown in sustainable forests and support the Forest
Stewardship Council, the leading international forest certification organization.
Our books displaying the FSC logo are printed on FSC certified paper.

For Teachers of Transcendental Meditation

TABLE *of* CONTENTS

Picture someone who teaches meditation, and I am probably not that person. I am often dressed in a suit, for one, and my offices are in Midtown Manhattan. I am not at all New Agey. I am a natural sceptic, and I am even more obsessed with science than I am with baseball, which is to say, *very*. I am not into woo-woo stuff. My friends have a running joke about me: 'How can a vegetarian be such a meat-and-potatoes guy?' I like things to be simple, practical, and thoroughly, unassailably logical.

And for more than forty-five years, teaching the Transcendental Meditation technique has been my full-time job. The technique comes from the oldest continuous meditation tradition in the world. There is no philosophy, change in lifestyle, or religion involved in its practice. For well over five thousand years, the TM technique was passed down from teacher to student, one to one: never in groups, never from a book. It has roots in the ancient noble warrior classes, where acting out of fear or anger brought disaster and defeat. Today it is for all of us who seek greater balance in life as well as more creativity, better health, less stress – and happiness.

Over those thousands of years, the TM technique has been honed to twenty minutes, twice a day: once in the morning, ideally before breakfast; and again in the late afternoon or early evening, ideally before dinner. You typically learn this meditation from a professionally trained teacher who will instruct you in a one-to-one session. He or she will give you your own mantra – a word or sound that has no meaning associated with it – and teach you how to think it properly, which means easily, effortlessly and silently. You'll learn that you don't need to push out thoughts, or watch your breath, or monitor sensations in your body, or visualize anything. You'll also learn that there is no need to sit in any particular position. You can sit up comfortably in a chair at home, at work, on a train or plane; on a park bench – basically, wherever it's comfortable. The morning session wakes up your brain and gives you energy and resilience so that the demands and challenges of the day don't stress you out. Then you meditate once again, ideally in the late afternoon or early evening before dinner, to start the next part of your day fresh. Twice a day, TM gives you a reset.

I have taught many thousands of people to meditate. My students are the leaders of Fortune 100 companies and are cashiers in small family shops. They go to colleges and urban schools. They are Christians, Jews, Buddhists, Muslims and Hindus, or they practise no religion whatsoever. They run the gamut from professional athletes to people living in homeless shelters. Whomever I am sitting across from – whether it's a CEO of one of the world's largest financial institutions or a single working mum with two young children at home or a veteran who hasn't slept more than two hours a night for months – they have the same look in their eyes when they come to me to talk about meditation. They are looking for something more; they are ready for a change.

I was in their shoes once, and I was perhaps more sceptical than any of them. In 1969 I was a university student with a nagging sense that there had to be something more I could be doing to be happier, healthier, more productive. I saw far too many people who had acquired the things that are supposed to make you that way, and yet they were often too stressed with too much worry, and, too often, unhappy. A friend whom I trusted, who had observed my own spiking stress levels from too much school pressure, suggested I might like Transcendental Meditation. I balked. I wasn't interested. Meditation wasn't even a word in my vocabulary. I was (and am) a very practical, down-to-earth, active kind of a guy. My trajectory was to go to law school so that I could run for public office and ultimately become a US senator. I wanted to help change the world. (Yes, we thought those things then.) Sitting around 'meditating' didn't fit into my life view.

But I wasn't sleeping well, and my memory was flagging, and I did respect my friend's opinion, so I decided to at least give TM a try. Despite my initial reticence and scepticism, I found the experience to be marked, significant, real. It was astonishingly easy to do, deeply relaxing, and yet incredibly energizing, like nothing I had experienced before. From the very start, I knew that, somehow, I wanted to teach this to people; and, in particular, I wanted to teach it to inner-city school kids. A few years later, in January 1972, I took a semester off from my studies and enrolled in a graduate-level five-month TM teacher training course led by Maharishi Mahesh Yogi, himself a university-trained physicist and the foremost meditation teacher of this generation. During the course, Maharishi and a team of brain scientists, physicians and psychologists explored ancient and modern insights into the science of consciousness, as well as the impact of stress and trauma on the brain and nervous system. We learned the unique mechanics of the TM practice and the role of this meditation for unfolding the seemingly limitless creativity and intelligence within the human mind, as well as its ability to address effectively many of society's intractable ills. Most importantly, Maharishi taught us the simple yet precise technique of how to personally teach any individual to *transcend* – to effortlessly access the deep stillness that lies within every human being – in a way that was tailored specifically for that person.

From his earliest days of teaching TM in the world in 1958, Maharishi focused on researching and understanding the science of Transcendental Meditation. He challenged doctors at Harvard, UCLA and other medical schools to study the neurophysiological changes both during and after the technique. The results are abundantly clear today. Since then, more than four hundred scientific studies have shown the wide-ranging benefits of the TM technique for improving brain and cognitive functioning, cardiovascular health and emotional wellbeing. These studies have been published in top peer-reviewed science journals, including the American Medical Association's *JAMA Internal Medicine*, and the American Heart Association's journals *Stroke* and *Hypertension*. (To be clear, it matters greatly that this research is peer-reviewed. Medical peer review means that experts are evaluating the credibility of the study, and also ensuring that the clinicians involved meet established standards of care.) The US National Institutes of Health has provided tens of millions of dollars to study TM's effects on stress and heart health, while the US Department of Defense has awarded several million dollars to study its impact on post-traumatic stress disorder (PTSD) in veterans returning from combat in Iraq and Afghanistan.

The change has taken time, but the Transcendental Meditation technique is now recognized as a powerful treatment and preventative modality for so many of the stress-based disorders of our time – as well as an immensely practical tool to markedly improve health and performance. In the same way that we now recognize the importance of exercise and eating healthy, the world has come a long way with regards to understanding the critical importance of meditation in general and Transcendental Meditation in particular.

That certainly was not always the case. When I first began my work, sometimes the fastest way to end a conversation was to say I was a meditation teacher. Now, if someone asks me what I do, they lean in as I say that I run a non-profit that teaches Transcendental Meditation in 35 countries all over the world. The person's eyes usually widen, and he or she says, 'Oh, I could really use that.'

So what happened? Why is there so much interest in meditation? I attribute it to a perfect storm of three factors:

One, we are living in an epidemic of stress. We face more toxic stress now than at any other time in history. It compromises the immune system, stunts cognitive and emotional development, and raises blood pressure, the latter of which puts tens of millions of people at risk for cardiovascular disease – the number one killer of our age. In fact, according to the British Heart Foundation, heart and circulatory diseases kill more than one in four people in the UK. In Australia, the Heart Foundation estimates that nearly one in three people die of heart and circulatory diseases. Toxic stress also helps fuel a challenging range of disorders: eating, sleeping, learning, obsessive-compulsive, bipolar and more. It speeds the ageing process and shortens life spans. Day to day, stress fills us with so much tension and anxiety that it is often difficult to even enjoy the little things that used to make us happy.

I travel a lot for my work, and I can see this stress in the faces of people I meet. No matter who they are, what they do, or where they come from, they tell me that too often they overreact to small irritants, much less life's bigger challenges. They admit recoiling from a mobile phone's incessant ring, and they awaken to a jammed email inbox with dread. It's not their imagination: stress, in fact, heightens our sensitivity to new stress triggers. In other words, stress begets more stress. Without any exaggeration – and to be brutally blunt about it – stress kills.

And now we are in constant contact, living in a 24/7 plugged-in world that never, ever stops. We are glutted by information, demands and sensory input. We are on an endless loop of requests to read, review, make a decision, keep, delete, reply, and move to the next request. The more success we achieve, the more high-stakes decisions we are forced to make.

Yes, a lot of people are seriously overworked, and yes, a lot of people don't like their jobs. But I also meet people all the time who love their work and relish pressure. They wish there were more hours in the day to get things done. People at the top of their game love to be challenged. But whether you love or hate your job, you can still pay the physical and emotional tolls of stress. You can enjoy your work but still struggle to do it effectively if it's hard to get out of bed because you wake up feeling worn out or dragged down by a relentless undercurrent of anxiety. Or maybe you wake up energized, but that energy wanes in the early afternoon, and even those cups of coffee don't give you the buzz you need to get through the day. Things that hadn't bothered you before are starting to. You don't remember things like you used to and it's tougher to concentrate for extended periods of time. For the first time, you find yourself getting tension headaches or relying on sleeping pills to make it through the night.

It's a downward spiral. You've read the diagnosis and the prognosis, and neither is pretty. Stress costs US businesses upward of $300 billion a year thanks to overworked employees becoming disengaged, drained, unfocused and burned out.[1] In the United Kingdom, stress is the most common reason employees take long-term sick leave – more than repetitive stress injuries, heart disease and cancer.[2] And in Japan, the government has officially classified toxic stress as a fatal phenomenon, with the Ministry of Health, Labour and Welfare collecting statistics on *karoshi* (death from overwork) since 1987.[3]

And we are starting our children on this path at younger and younger ages. I recently visited a classroom of seven- and eight-year-olds. I looked at all these little faces as I explained the work I do. In gentle terms, I talked about adults feeling stressed, and I asked casually, 'How many of you feel stressed?'

Every single hand went up. Children! I was stunned. Stress doesn't affect just those kids who deal with scarcity and violence and unstable home lives. Paediatricians are seeing more and more children from more affluent homes with adult levels of anxiety linked to performance pressure.

So we know we have a problem, and we know we need a solution. The second reason for the surge of interest in meditation is that there is no magic pill to save us from the epidemic. That's usually where we go for the answer: to the medicine cabinet. Sure, there is a zillion-pound treasure chest of drugs to manage all those crippling stress-related ailments. We take pills to sleep, more pills to calm nerves or enhance performance at work. Or we go 'over the counter,' so to speak, to mask the symptoms by drinking multiple cups of coffee to make it through the day. Then maybe several glasses of wine to slow down for the evening. And kids, at earlier and earlier ages, are already reliant on antidepressant and antianxiety medications to control attention disorders.

But, in truth, we get little from the pharmaceutical companies to actually prevent or cure toxic stress. Drugs often prove ineffective – and those that do work can come with hazardous side effects. As the stakes get higher and higher, more and more people are naturally drawn to look elsewhere for a solution.

Which brings us to the third reason for the explosion of interest in meditation: science, science and more science. There is so much evidence validating the benefits of meditation that even the most sceptical among us has to (perhaps begrudgingly) acknowledge that something significant, something important, is going on when we meditate.

But what does it mean to 'meditate'? There is so much buzz about meditation and 'mindfulness' in the popular culture, but there is also so much confusion. What is it, exactly?

When I talk about meditation, I use an analogy. I tell my students, You are in a little boat in the middle of the Atlantic Ocean, and for as far as you can see, there is an expanse of blue.

But all of a sudden, the water begins to get choppy, and you find yourself surrounded by huge, thirty-foot waves. You could easily think, 'The whole ocean is in upheaval!'

The *whole* ocean? Not really. Because if you could look at a cross section downward, you would see that only the surface is in turmoil. The Atlantic is several miles deep, and at its depth, the ocean is very, very calm. Down there is an unbounded expanse of peace and tranquility, entirely undisturbed by the turbulence above.

Like the waves on the surface of the ocean, the surface of the mind can be active – even noisy and turbulent. Some characterize the surface of the mind as the 'monkey mind.' I like to call it the 'gotta-gotta-gotta' mind. The hyperactive type A mind is always thinking, 'I gotta do this. I gotta do that. I gotta call him. I gotta call her. I gotta make a list. Then I gotta find the list. Then I gotta make a new list. I gotta slow down. I gotta get going. I gotta get to sleep, I gotta get up.'

Sound familiar?

Pretty much everyone knows the experience. And pretty much everyone has had the thought, at one time or another, 'I'd like a break from the mental noise; from the constant mental chatter. I'd like some inner stillness, some inner clarity, some inner creativity, some inner focus, some inner peace.'

The operative word there is *inner*. And the question is, is there such a thing as an *inner*? And if so, how do we get there?

'How we get there' has been the domain of meditation since times immemorial. Meditation has long been associated with ideas of inner equanimity, clarity, focus, creativity, strength. But, again, there are so many different types of meditation. Are they all the same? Do they all work?

I have been practising and teaching meditation for a

very long time. In the early days of my practice, the words 'I meditate' – if they were taken seriously – would often be translated to mean 'I jog,' 'I listen to soothing music,' 'I follow my thoughts as they come and go,' 'I breathe deeply,' or 'I repeat a sound in my head.' Everything was grouped under the big-top tent of 'meditating.'

But now that assumption no longer holds up. From brain science we know that there are basically three different approaches to meditation. This is because every discrete experience changes the brain in a discrete way: your brain responds differently if you listen to classical music or electronic music, if you watch a romantic comedy or a horror movie. In the same way, scientists have found marked, and important, differences in the way the brain functions during these different practices. Likewise, the cardiovascular, respiratory and nervous systems each respond differently to each meditation technique.

Understanding the three approaches is important because each requires different degrees of effort and difficulty to practise; each impacts the brain differently; and each produces different outcomes for the health of mind and body.

These three techniques are Focused Attention, Open Monitoring, and Automatic Self-Transcending.[4]

Focused Attention includes the classic depiction of

meditation in popular culture: someone sitting upright, cross-legged on a floor or pillow, eyes closed and absorbed in a state of unwavering, deep inner peace. If you've ever gone to a yoga class, you've likely encountered this approach. Thoughts are seen as the disrupter of mental calm, so you are asked to minimize – or better yet, stop – your wandering 'monkey' mind, to clear your mind of thoughts.

To return to the ocean analogy, trying to clear your mind of thoughts is like trying to stop every wave on the surface of the ocean. It takes moment-to-moment hypervigilance, and for many people, it is a lot of work. Some even give up, insisting, 'I can't do it. Meditation isn't for me.'

How do Focused Attention techniques impact the brain? One way to tell is through electroencephalography (EEG), which measures the electrical activity of the brain. EEG readouts measured while test subjects practise Focused Attention show that these techniques enliven gamma brain waves in the left prefrontal cortex, the brain's decision maker. This means that the electrical activity in the brain reaches a frequency per second of about 20 to 50 hertz (Hz), or cycles per second. You see a similar result when a student concentrates on a mathematical problem – which makes sense, because gamma waves are found when one is engaged in a challenging task.

14

In contrast to attempting to clear the mind of thoughts, the second category of meditation, Open Monitoring, also known as mindfulness, is about learning to observe thoughts dispassionately, without judgement, as they come and go. This is because thoughts themselves are not seen as the potential disrupter of calm, but rather it is the content or meaning of thoughts that can disrupt. So you learn to remain calm, unaffected and present even when your mind is percolating with thoughts about annoyances at work or a longstanding argument with your partner.

Back to the ocean analogy. Now you're in that little boat, and instead of trying to stop the waves, you are observing them rise and fall without emotion. In the process, you're generating theta brain waves, with the electrical patterns slowing to about 6 to 8 Hz, close to the onset of dreams. Theta waves are associated with creativity, daydreaming and memory tasks. Several studies on mindfulness practices, many of which are included in the Opening Monitoring classification, also show alpha-2 brain waves (10 to 12 Hz) in the back of the brain. These waves are associated with turning off brain areas – in this case, the visual system – and beta waves (16 to 20 Hz), which means that you are actively engaged in directing your attention. In addition, neural imaging shows that such mindfulness practices activate the anterior cingulate cortices, which are involved in emotions, learning and memory.

Open Monitoring can help you become more present and centered during stressful experiences. It can help calm your amygdala – the area of the brain that governs emotions and emotional behaviour – so that you don't overreact to a situation. You can take a few minutes, breathe deeply, conduct a scan of how you are reacting, calm yourself, and reenter the fray. For many, it is a useful and practical coping tool.

Open Monitoring is a cognitive process like Focused Attention. By definition, it keeps your attention in the present moment – on the level of attending to the surface thinking level of the mind.

I have been fortunate to learn Focused Attention and Open Monitoring from some of the best instructors, so I know firsthand that there is value to both practices. But the one that I have practised regularly for nearly fifty years – the one that I find the easiest to do and that delivers the most immediate and long-term benefits to mind and body – is the third type: Automatic Self-Transcending.

Transcendental Meditation is in this category. Let's return to the ocean analogy yet again: there are active, often turbulent waves on the surface, but there is calm at its depth. In the same way, we hypothesize that while the mind is active on the surface, deep within is a level that is calm yet alert; silent yet wide awake. The ancient meditation texts refer to it as the 'source of thought' or 'pure consciousness' – a field of limitless creativity, intelligence and energy within. Scientists give it a more clinical description: a state of 'restful alertness.' It is there. Deep within. Right now and at all times. Believe it or not. The problem is, we have lost access to it.

The purpose of TM is to open the door to this unbounded field. There is no concentration or control of the mind; nothing guided; no suggestion or passive observation. Instead, TM simply allows the active-thinking mind to settle down to its own state of inner stillness at the deepest level of awareness, one that actually *transcends*, or goes beyond, all thoughts and feelings. It is your own quiet inner self, before you start thinking and creating and planning and making lists and deciding and worrying and celebrating. It's always been there, within you. It just gets lost or overshadowed easily by the constant noise and distractions of the day.

In the context of the ocean analogy, we don't try to control those turbulent waves on the surface, and we don't watch them dispassionately, either. We simply access the calm at the ocean's depth.

It's like a sprinter who decelerates from a fast run,

to a slow jog, to a leisurely walk, to standing still, to sitting down. Same guy, just different degrees of activity. Easy.

EEG readouts and brain imaging reveal that Transcendental Meditation strengthens the neural connections between the different areas of the brain, including within the prefrontal cortex, to promote better learning and decision making.[5] It calms the amygdala, the sensitive stress alarm centre in your brain, which is important because a hyperaroused amygdala makes you overreact to both small glitches and big challenges in your day. Or it can immobilize you, making you shy away from new but doable challenges.

During TM practice, your brain wave signature shifts to alpha-1 (8 to 10 Hz), which is seen mostly in the front of the brain, the prefrontal cortex. Alpha-1 indicates that the mind is deeply rested, reflective and wide awake. TM activates the default mode network, a large-scale network in the brain that is tied to improved creativity and decision making. It also acts on the nucleus accumbens, the brain's reward centre, which is associated with happiness and even euphoria. At the same time, there is increased blood flow to the brain, which means your brain is getting more nourishment. Finally, and uniquely, the body gains a profound state of rest and relaxation that goes along with heightened mental alertness. This means that TM provides more than just rest. It produces deep rest and inner alertness, together – or, as I said, a unique state of restful alertness.

The experience of restful alertness triggers a constellation of neurophysiological and biochemical changes in your body, including a reduction in high blood pressure; a decrease in galvanic skin response, which is an indicator of deep physiological calm; a 30 per cent reduction in the stress hormone cortisol; and an increase of serotonin, which is the neurotransmitter, or brain chemical, associated with mood balance and happiness. Your body does this automatically as your brain functions in a more integrated, coherent style. And here's the important thing: these effects are cumulative. The benefits of meditation last throughout the day, many hours after you've finished your twenty minutes.

My friend and student Dr Peter Attia sometimes prescribes TM to those who come to his offices in New York City and San Diego. Dr Attia was a surgeon at Johns Hopkins Hospital, a surgical oncology fellow at the National Cancer Institute, and has been mentored by the foremost lipidologists, endocrinologists, gynaecologists, sleep physiologists, and longevity scientists in North America. This ultrafit doctor is so consumed by his interest in human physiology that he wears a continuous glucose monitor 24/7 and a device to accurately measure his sleep quality through heart rate variability every night. He is his own case study in the pursuit of physiological excellence. His passion is his practice, Attia Medical, where his focus is the applied science of longevity and optimal performance. His clients are superstars in their fields; the kind of people working at peak performance. Now many are doing TM at his suggestion.

'I have this joke in my practice,' Dr Attia says. 'I don't have anything against a Toyota, but I don't enjoy tuning Toyotas – I want to tune up Ferraris.' The metaphor describes his patients perfectly. 'When you are racing at the limit of the machine, like a Ferrari,' he says, 'everything matters. It's just sometimes more obvious when you make an improvement under high-stress conditions, and by stress, I don't mean physiological stress. I mean aggregate stress, like the stress of the machine.'

Most of his patients, male and female, are total alphas who want to work longer and harder, start more companies, sit on more corporate boards – basically, change the world in one way or another. While the challenges that his patients thrive on get them on the front page of the *Wall Street Journal*, the accompanying stress of their work can kill them. 'If the model is that the only way we're going to fix someone is to prevent all the stressors, I think we're playing a lot of whack-a-mole,' he told me.

'A smarter strategy is, "Can we fix how you *respond* to stress?" Meditation, broadly speaking, is a tool. And in my opinion, TM is a great application of that tool.'

Case-in-point: Jonathon Fitzgerald has been a leader in the retail world of fashion, home and general merchandise in the UK and globally for over twenty-five years, including serving as the CEO of Mamas and Papas, the baby products, furniture and maternity wear firm. Jonathon has practised TM throughout the entire tenure.

'If I wasn't meditating I imagine I would be far more susceptible to stress and anger. I would be anxious a lot. TM gives me resilience and energy to deal with my very busy and stressful schedule. But the fact is I am meditating regularly and the reality is I would not have reached the level of success I have in my career without it,' Jonathon says.

With his encouragement his family meditates as well and that has brought a much deeper dimension to his personal life: 'My relationships are more connected, more satisfying. I've watched my wife and children and friends grow from their own meditation practice. TM is the best gift I've ever given anyone.'

Just about everyone I teach – the money manager navigating an unstable market, the parent holding two jobs to make ends meet, or the graduate school student feeling the pressure of an impending doctoral dissertation – says they want to continue to perform at higher and higher levels. At the same time, they don't want to be stressed out, staying awake all night. Meditation, properly understood and practised, addresses both of these concerns in one stroke by accessing the field of silence, creativity and energy within. That is the strength in stillness.

You will see that this book is composed of three pillars. In the first, I explain exactly what the TM technique is, how it works, what it does, and where it comes from. The second pillar will take you through what you can expect as you learn the practice, and there we will go deeper into medical and brain research showing exactly how TM heals your body, improves your reactions to stress, and optimizes brain function.

The third pillar serves as an inspiration and guide as you start on this path to develop your full creative innermost self. In this final pillar you'll meet people from all walks of life – CEOs, artists, veterans and students – who have seen TM change their lives for the better. I will also share more of my own journey, and talk about what the TM technique has done for me. Throughout, I present Meditative Moments where you will hear directly from people about what it feels like to meditate, and more importantly, how it makes them feel throughout the rest of the day.

——————— · ———————

MEDITATIVE MOMENT
The Secret Weapon

Orin Snyder is not afraid of the word win. Considered one of the top trial lawyers in the world, Orin has represented Facebook and Bob Dylan, handled billion-dollar lawsuits, and earned his rep as the 'deadliest lawyer in tech.' We met recently in his corner office at the law firm Gibson Dunn, high up in Manhattan's MetLife Building, to talk about how TM has helped him become an even fiercer advocate for his clients.

I've always been active and athletic, but two years ago, I started weight training around the same time I started meditating. I see them as close relatives. If you regularly lift weights for forty minutes a day, you will develop physical musculature. That investment of forty minutes completely transforms your body. The same is true for TM: if you meditate for twenty minutes twice a day, you will develop what I like to call the 'chill muscle' that right now is inert in so many of us.

I learned to meditate first and foremost so I could have more calm in my inner life. I wanted to worry less. Meditation delivered — and has been a game-changer in terms of my own personal happiness. But my regular meditation practice also produced unanticipated benefits in my professional life. TM makes me more effective as an advocate for my clients because it makes me less reactive and gives me enhanced clarity.

Across all industries and professional endeavours, meditation can serve as a potent secret weapon. I call it the X factor in achieving transcendence in your professional life. TM helps get you to the next level in your professional pursuits by strengthening your focus and resolve. I often hear people say that TM is only for people who are interested in a serene interior life or a world of communal living in some post-utopian society free of conflict or competition. That is a myth.

I'll give you an example. I often have to fly to the West Coast for work. Last year alone I took fifteen or more trips. I usually have to execute a particular assignment on arrival, whether it's a court hearing, board meeting, or client presentation. Often I'm exhausted, and I always have multiple demands on my time and on my mental focus.

Recently I flew to California for an important meeting. I woke up at four in the morning for a six o'clock flight, and for seven hours on the plane I worked intensely to prepare a presentation. I arrived, the presentation went smoothly, and I turned around and got right back on a red-eye flight back to New York that same day. I was utterly exhausted, but instead of sleeping, I worked to prepare for another meeting the next morning. I was cramming without much sleep, and while I landed at JFK at dawn prepared substantively, I was spent.

I went home to shower, shave and put on a new suit. I got in a taxi uptown and headed to midtown for the meeting at my office. I could have fallen asleep right then and there, but it was obvious what I needed to do: meditate. I was drawn to it like a dog to a bone. Happily, traffic on Park Avenue cooperated, and we hit massive gridlock. Despite honking horns and cursing taxi drivers, I closed my eyes and meditated deeply for twenty minutes.

I remember the moment of getting out of the taxi vividly, even physically. I flung open the door on Park Avenue, and when I walked onto the street, I felt alive and rejuvenated in a way that startled me. I had been practising TM for enough time that I had developed a stockpile of calm that I accessed when I went inward for those twenty minutes. And the dividends were immediate: my body rewarded me with energy and clarity. That reservoir of musculature that I developed through all of my meditations was there to be activated.

I nailed the meeting and was refreshed for that whole day. Critically, I did the second meditation that afternoon in an empty conference room. I needed more of a kick start, another dose of energy. I went home that night and went right to bed. But that taxi meditation was my source of energy, focus, and ultimately success. Now, I am not saying you have to keep my crazy schedule to benefit from TM. Transcendental Meditation is good for everyone.

———————————— • ————————————

Kate Erman is also an attorney who has seen great benefits from Transcendental Meditation. Kate comes from Sydney, Australia. She has been practising commercial law for 11 years and Transcendental Meditation for six years. She tells her story: 'I have been interested in meditation as a means to combat stress and anxiety for a very long time. I tried many techniques over the years and, although I found them helpful for a short period, the concentration required was very hard work and ultimately not sustainable. I was looking for something that I could easily and effortlessly incorporate into my day – and fortunately I found this in TM.

'For as long as I can remember I have been plagued with a gnawing anxiety and interminable low moods from job pressures and challenging personal relationships. Within just three months of regular practice I started to notice that these feelings melted away. I am happier and life is smoother. I can now appreciate what's good about the moment, wherever I am and no matter what the circumstances. And it just keeps getting better!'

PILLAR *one*

A WORKING DEFINITION

What exactly is Transcendental Meditation? To define TM, I always start with three adjectives: simple, natural and effortless.

TM is simple not because it is simplistic or a beginner's meditation but rather because there is an elegant simplicity to the practice.

It's natural because there is no suggestion or manipulation involved.

It's effortless because there is no concentration or control required.

Here is what TM is not:

It's not a religion. Nearly eight million people of all religions, as well as people who have no religion, have learned TM over the past sixty years.

It's not a philosophy. TM is a technique you learn and then practise on your own; nothing else.

It's not a change in lifestyle. Once you learn to meditate, you don't have to change your diet and suddenly start eating tofu (unless you like it!).

And finally, there is nothing to believe in. You can be 100 per cent sceptical, and it doesn't matter. The technique works equally well whether you believe in it or not.

TM is not an acquired skill that you will get 'better' at after weeks or months of practice. You master it in a few hours over a few days, and then it's yours for the rest of your life.

As I mentioned earlier, TM is practised for twenty minutes, twice a day, sitting up comfortably in a chair (or on your bed or wherever you can sit up comfortably), with your eyes closed. It can be practised in the privacy of your home but can be done just as easily on a train or airplane or in a car (as long as someone else is driving!). It is a silent technique, so you are not going to disturb anyone while you meditate. If you feel an itch, by all means scratch it. I once taught a record company executive, and when I said he could move during his meditation, his eyes actually welled up with tears of relief. For decades, he had worked hard trying to master meditation techniques that required concentration and control of the mind and body. He always felt like a failure if he had too many thoughts or needed to scratch an itch or move his leg to get more comfortable.

Not only that, but should you feel sleepy at any time during the meditation, you don't need to fight it. It's fine. If you do fall asleep because you're tired, it will be usually for a minute or two, and then you'll awaken rested and refreshed and continue with your practice. It just means your body needed the extra deep rest. Such moments are part of the meditation.

Perhaps the idea of meditating appeals to you, but the reality of trying to sit still for twenty minutes sounds too daunting, if not altogether impossible. Well, you can. I teach ten-year-old kids with attention deficit hyperactivity disorder (ADHD), who previously could not sit with their eyes closed for more than thirty seconds, and they love it. If they can do it, you can, too.

Why do so many people think that meditation is difficult? The answer is an unfortunate misunderstanding about the nature of the mind. For a long time, the prevailing attitude has been that thoughts are the enemy of meditation – distracting, disturbing and diminishing the effects – and therefore must be minimized, or altogether eliminated. I taught Oprah Winfrey to meditate. She told me she thought the same thing. She said that she kept failing in meditation because she had so many thoughts she could not stop. After her first experience with Transcendental Meditation, she was visibly relieved. 'That is so human-friendly,' she said of the very forgiving nature of the practice. Oprah was so pleased with her experience that she asked us to teach all four hundred of her team members at both Harpo, her production company, and Oprah Winfrey Network.

Let's go through the basic principles of how TM works.

Unlike other meditation practices, thoughts are part of the process in TM. There is no need to control your monkey mind because, in fact, your mind is not a monkey that needs controlling. It is not wandering aimlessly because your mind is not wandering at all.

It was Maharishi's insight that the natural tendency of the mind is not to wander without direction but rather to seek something more satisfying, more charming; greater knowledge, more happiness. And this insight is at the core of understanding not only how TM works but also how it differs from other forms of meditation.

Imagine that you are sitting in a room, listening to some pretty bad music when all of a sudden some unbelievably great music comes on in another room. It's the best music you've heard in a long time. So where does your attention automatically go? To the great music, obviously. You want to turn down the bad music and turn up the good.

Or you are at a reception before a dinner party, stuck in a corner, listening to someone you don't really know drone on about something you really don't care about. Your mind is going numb. Then suddenly you overhear, just a few feet away, a small group of people having a really interesting conversation. Now, you try to be polite to the person standing in front of you by maintaining eye contact, but your attention keeps being drawn away to the more engaging discussion.

Or, finally, you go on holiday and bring two books with you. One book is so boring you can't get beyond the first page. The other book is so absorbing that you read for hours without noticing the time.

These three familiar experiences all have one thing in common: your mind is drawn naturally to something more satisfying. There's no deliberation or intellectualisation, no pause to consider options or weigh the pros and cons, for example, of which music you prefer. If the music is absolutely great, your mind automatically goes there.

In the relentless search for satisfaction or happiness, the mind is drawn outward, through the senses, into the environment. You try a new movie or restaurant or holiday spot. You buy some new clothes or meet up with a new friend. In these cases, happiness comes from an external experience. It's nice, it's enjoyable – for as long as it lasts. But it's temporal, fleeting. The holiday is over, the film ends, and your friend goes home. And then you are inexorably drawn outward to find the next 'happiness.'

However, there is a field of satisfaction and happiness that does not fluctuate, that is not fleeting, that surpasses anything 'outer.' And that is to be found at the quietest, deepest level of the thinking mind. Transcendental Meditation bridges the surface with the depth. It makes use of the mind's natural tendency to seek more satisfaction and then gives the attention an inward direction, so that instantly, automatically and effortlessly the attention is drawn within. The active thinking mind settles down towards the most satisfying level of awareness. This is the experience of the 'inner' that meditation texts have extolled throughout the ages.

How do you get there? With a *mantra*, which is a word or sound that serves as a vehicle to facilitate the process of silently settling down from surface to depth, from noise to stillness. The mantra has no meaning associated with it, and according to ancient meditation texts its effects are known to be positive and life supporting. Its sole purpose is to help the mind access that inner calm without effort.

How do you get a mantra in Transcendental Meditation? The same way you would have gotten one for over five thousand years. From a specially trained teacher. He or she will give you your mantra and then teach you how to use it properly – naturally and effortlessly – without any concentration or control of the mind. You will learn the subtle mechanics of how to give the attention of your 'gotta-gotta' mind an inward direction so that automatically you begin to settle down and transcend into stillness. You will also learn how to deal with the steady influx of thoughts, outer noises, feeling sleepy, wanting to scratch an itch, and so on. (I will discuss this in more detail later in the book.) Your teacher will be with you, and you alone, to answer every question as it arises.

I used to hear this a lot: 'Why do I need a teacher?' 'Why can't I do this on my own?' Here's a story. As a 12-year-old kid, I used to attend a Boy Scout camp in California's High Sierra Mountains during the summer. One searing hot July morning, we took a twenty-mile hike that included spectacular wide-open mountain vistas as well as some rocky terrain and thick woods. We were led by an older Eagle Scout, a guy named Bruce Wagner (yes, I still remember his name), who had walked the trail many times for many years. Bruce knew every twist and turn, hitch and gully along the way. We flew through the twenty miles. It was challenging and fun and incredibly satisfying. Now, when I look back, could I have made my way on my own? Maybe. Although as I recall, the signposts were pretty confusing at points. What I do know is that Bruce was there as a guide every step of the way. He helped a ton. I was grateful for his help. He was a great teacher.

We want a properly trained teacher to instruct our children in maths and teach them how to swim or play piano. We want a properly trained doctor to diagnose our ailments and prescribe remedies. So why not a properly trained teacher to guide us with our meditation, not just to be there when we learn but also to be there should any question need answering, or a refresher be helpful, throughout our entire life?

As I've said, I have been a teacher for more than forty-five years. I have taught thousands of people, including a whole lot of sceptics. Each person who comes to learn is unique. Each has his or her own life experiences, doubts, questions, pace of learning, etc. I constantly marvel at the precision and effectiveness of the steps of instruction to teach a person to meditate. And how easy it is for anyone to practise the technique, once learned properly.

The ease of learning was confirmed by a 2017 study, which found that individuals practising TM for just one month reported the same frequency of transcendent experiences as individuals practising for five years.[1] So whether you are new to the practice or seasoned in TM, transcending – going beyond the chatter of the mind to increasingly quieter, more refined levels of thought – is natural to the practice because the ability to transcend is not an acquired skill that requires a lot of effort. In fact, it requires no effort at all.

Understanding How Transcendental Meditation Works

1. The mind has different levels: the surface levels of the thinking mind are active, often excited, and sometimes heated, while the deeper levels are calmer and more expansive. The deepest level is, by nature, most satisfying.

2. It's the nature of the mind to be drawn effortlessly to fields of greater satisfaction.

3. TM gives the attention an inward direction, and, through the proper use of a mantra, the mind naturally and effortlessly settles down to its own quiet, peaceful, transcendent state of awareness.

4. This experience produces a unique state of restful alertness, which is at the core of the constellation of neurophysiological changes to mind, body and behaviour.

*　　*　　*

'Who was Maharishi Mahesh Yogi?' is a question I am frequently asked by the press. How did a monk with a background in physics but who was living in seclusion in the high Himalayas, manage to bring meditation to millions of people starting in the 1950s and 1960s, when the whole idea of meditation was often dismissed as nonsense? Here is a very short history.

After graduating from India's Allahabad University with a degree in physics in 1941, Maharishi had the rare opportunity to work and study closely with his teacher, Brahmananda Saraswati, also known as Guru Dev, for thirteen years. Guru Dev was considered the foremost scientist of consciousness from the Vedic tradition of his time. After Guru Dev's passing in 1953, Maharishi retired to the small village of Uttarkashi in the foothills of India's Himalayas. There he went into silence for two years, living in solitude by the Ganges River. In 1955 he set out to travel alone, teaching the meditation technique that he had learned from his teacher – and that had been handed down for thousands of years from one great meditation master to the next.

In those early days in India, Maharishi's message – that meditation was simple, effortless and non-religious, and should be available to all – met with resistance in some quarters, particularly among certain people who felt meditation should be an elite practice, one that required exhaustive discipline, hard work and austerity over decades in order to begin to master its arcane skills.

In contrast, Maharishi said that meditation is everyone's birthright. You don't have to be a recluse, wear colourful robes, sit in a rigid manner, or eat a particular diet to master the practice and benefit from the results. You can be of any class or caste and meditate. If the field of silence exists deep within the mind, it exists for everyone, no matter a person's education, religion, belief system, age, profession, or lifestyle.

Freeing meditation of all those trappings, Maharishi brought his scientist's perspective to the teaching of the technique. Soon after he arrived for the first time in the United States in January 1959, Maharishi began meeting with scientists, urging them to study the neurophysiological effects of Transcendental Meditation. He emphasized that TM, like any other recognized medicine or treatment modality, would stand on its scientifically verified benefits.

The first clinical trials, held at Harvard Medical School and UCLA Medical School in 1968, were published in the journal *Science* in 1970 and *Scientific American* magazine in 1972, respectively. In the Harvard study, researchers led by physiologist Dr Robert Keith Wallace, investigated the unique changes in brain wave patterns during TM and correlated them with reductions in the metabolic rate. Dr Wallace and others proposed this meditative state to be a 'fourth major state of consciousness,' distinct from waking, sleeping and dreaming. Those first two studies opened the floodgates on TM research and also helped to fuel extensive research on other meditation techniques.

In those beginning years, Maharishi was portrayed in the popular press differently from the man I had the opportunity to work with for more than forty years. During the 1960s, a monk with long hair wearing a white dhoti was an anomaly. The press first took notice in August 1967, when Maharishi was giving a talk at the Hilton Hotel in London. Three young guys walked in, followed by a lot of reporters. It was three-quarters of the Beatles: Paul McCartney, John Lennon and George Harrison. (Ringo Starr was with his newborn son, Jason.) The next day, Maharishi taught all four Beatles to meditate during a course in Wales. They all continued the practice throughout their lives. In an interview with journalist David Frost, George Harrison brought his gift of words to describe the experience of TM: 'The whole idea is to transcend to the subtlest level of thought. And the mantra becomes subtler and subtler until finally you transcend even the mantra. Then you find yourself at this level of pure consciousness.

'When you reach that point,' George continued, 'it's

deep down there beyond normal experience, and that level is timeless, spaceless, without identity. So you even don't know how long you have been there. You just have the contact, and then you go back up to the gross level, to this level.'

George Harrison had described what the ancient meditation texts of all cultures have extolled for millennia: transcendence.

Here are two questions I get a lot: How is Transcendental Meditation different from 'regular' meditation? And what does the word *transcendental* in Transcendental Meditation mean? Let's start with the first question. *Meditation* means thinking. So different meditations utilize different techniques of thinking. As I said, there is thinking that keeps the mind focused and controlled (Focused Attention), thinking that keeps the mind in the present (Open Monitoring), and thinking that allows the mind to access inner stillness, or transcend (Automatic Self-Transcending).

So what does *transcendental* mean? What is transcendence?

For some people, *transcendence* has a strange sound to it – almost mystical or otherworldly. *Merriam-Webster's Collegiate Dictionary* defines transcendence as 'extending or lying beyond the limits of ordinary experience.'

In truth, it's not strange at all. In fact, we seek transcendence all the time – whenever we seek to break boundaries, whenever we test our limits. We want to run faster, jump higher, learn more, earn more, see more, feel more. We love routine but, over time, it can stifle, suffocate. We seek change. We step out of our comfort zone in large and small ways. We take a new job that is more challenging and creative. We do something we've never done before such as join a theatre group or take a spin class. We go to an exotic location for a holiday. We experiment with new restaurants, new cuisines. We do something that injects the extraordinary into the ordinary. We feel excited, alive, energized. But only for a while, because eventually extraordinary can become ordinary, too. We're seeking transcendence, but it doesn't come simply by making changes in our daily routine on a horizontal level, like replacing one wave with another on the surface of the ocean. Real transcendence is more profound than that. It's vertical. It's going *beyond* the waves and accessing the unbounded stillness that lies deep within. And when you experience that pure stillness within yourself, at the source of thought, even for a moment, you remember it for a lifetime.

Great athletes call it the zone. The crowd noise and the big-game pressure dissipate as they focus on the match. What these gifted performers are left with is the game itself, as if in silent slow motion – a seamless sequence of flawless events in time.

Tennis great Billie Jean King captured her experiences of the zone eloquently in her autobiography *Billie Jean*. 'I can almost feel it coming,' she writes. 'It usually happens on one of those days when everything is just right, when the crowd is large and enthusiastic and my concentration is so perfect it almost seems as though I'm able to transport myself beyond the turmoil on the court to some place of total peace and calm. I know where the ball is on every shot, and it always looks as big and well defined as a basketball. Just a huge thing I couldn't miss if I wanted to. I've got perfect control of the match, my rhythm and movements are excellent, and everything's just in total balance. It's a perfect combination of a violent action taking place in an atmosphere of total tranquility ... And when it happens, I want to stop the match and grab the microphone and shout, "That's what it's all about."'

But it's not just for athletes. Brain surgeons, trial lawyers, schoolteachers, musicians, and stay-at-home mums can experience transcendence as well. In fact, it can happen, to one degree or another, to anyone. Like when you hug your newborn child, and time slips away. Or when you connect deeply with a beloved partner, and you are enveloped in a moment that seems to last forever. It's the kid in the garden shooting hoops when magically, when no one is looking, he or she hits ten impossible shots in a row: *swish, swish, swish*. Or the author who has been battling writer's block suddenly finds all the right words flowing, page after page.

These are glimpses of the zone, or transcendence. Different experiences at different times but all sharing the commonality of action infused with silence – effortless, timeless and satisfying way beyond the norm. The important thing is it starts from inside. You take note of these moments because they are meaningful and indescribably fulfilling.

Some of the greatest poets have done justice to the experience. The closest description I have seen in writing is William Wordsworth's 'Lines Composed a Few Miles Above Tintern Abbey':

> *[T]hat serene and blessed mood,*
> *In which the affections gently lead us on,*
> *Until the breath of this corporeal frame,*
> *And even the motion of our human blood*
> *Almost suspended, we are laid asleep*
> *In body, and become a living soul:*
> *While with an eye made quiet by the power*
> *Of harmony, and the deep power of joy,*
> *We see into the life of things.*

But for the rest of us non-poets, transcendence can be a challenge to put into words. What does it feel like? It's like trying to describe happiness in words. Or telling someone who has never eaten a kiwi what it tastes like. 'No, it doesn't exactly taste like an orange, a peach, or a strawberry . . .' You can try to say what it is: 'The bright-green flesh has a juicy texture and sweetness, and the tiny seeds within can add just the slightest grit . . .' But you will never fully convey the experience precisely through words. It must be experienced firsthand.

The Transcendental Meditation technique has many purposes: reduce stress, clear the mind, raise performance. But foremost among them is to experience transcendence. And not on rare, once-or-twice-in-a-lifetime occasions but whenever you want, to one degree or another, every day. Does it always feel like the ways that Billie Jean King or William Wordsworth describe it? Of course not. Sometimes the experience in medita-tion is profound; oftentimes it can seem mundane. But each time you meditate, even if your mind is filled with a million thoughts, you do settle down toward levels of the mind that are deeper, quieter, more satisfying. And when you do that, the equanimity you experience during meditation naturally comes out to be lived more and more in every moment of your life. And that is a very good description of the zone.

———————— . ————————

MEDITATIVE MOMENT
I Love Energy

Jerry Seinfeld started TM in 1972, when he was eighteen. In 2009 we met backstage for the first time at Radio City Music Hall during a benefit concert for the David Lynch Foundation to raise the funds to teach one million at-risk youth around the world to meditate. We connected, remained friends, and the next thing I knew, several years had passed, and I was at his home on Long Island teaching his family to meditate.

We were all hanging out in the kitchen one day, and Jerry mentioned that he meditates every afternoon. I asked about his morning meditation. He gave me a quizzical look and said he'd been meditating only once a day. But, smart guy that he is, he suddenly realized that maybe he was getting only half the benefits – maybe even less. In his unique, Seinfeldian way, he recently shared what doubling his daily TM sessions did for him.

I stopped doing my morning TM pretty early because I didn't understand the value of getting out of bed and then ... resting! I had trouble with that concept: get out of bed, now meditate, and rest some more. But I was very regular with my afternoon meditation.

Then I started doing the television series in which I was the star of the show, the executive producer and head writer. I did casting and editing for twenty-two to twenty-four episodes per season on network television for nine years. That's a lot of work, and I'm pretty much a regular guy. I'm not one of those crazy people who have endless, boundless energy.

So I'm a normal guy, but that was not a normal situation. Every day, when everybody would have lunch, I would meditate. Then we'd go back to work, and I would eat afterwards. That was how I survived the nine years. Those twenty minutes of TM in the middle of the day saved me.

Now, I know everybody's life is hard and every job is hard, but when it's your name on the show, the pressure is intense. The show got successful, and everybody expected each week to be better than the last. I loved every second, but it was a lot of pressure and a lot of work, and I never could've accomplished it without TM. But remember, I was meditating only once a day.

When you reminded me about the morning meditation, it changed everything. I'm a sixty-three-year-old guy with little kids – and now, because of TM, I'm functioning at a level that I really did not think was possible for someone my age. I get up at six in the morning and meditate before my kids get up to have breakfast. I like watching them eat cereal, and I like the little milk dribbling down their chins.

BOB ROTH

When I tell people I get up to meditate, they ask me how it feels. It doesn't feel like much of anything. I don't understand it either, but here's the difference: at one o'clock later that day, I'm no longer shot. My head does not hit the desk like it used to. Being a writer is a big part of being a comedian, and writing is a very exhaustive activity. I used to literally collapse in the middle of writing and have to lie on the couch and take a nap. Now, at one o'clock, I'm feeling good from my morning meditation seven hours earlier. I just sail through the day, and I have my second TM at three or four in the afternoon.

The unfortunate thing about being a lifelong meditator is there's no control group to look at what would've happened if I didn't do it. But I do know I am a lot better when I'm not exhausted. I love energy. I pursue it, and I want it. I think this is the reason that I am so enthusiastic about TM.

I also know that had I been meditating twice a day all these years, *Seinfeld* would still be on the air!

———————— • ————————

Sam Taylor-Johnson is another creative force who has benefitted greatly from her meditation practice. Sam describes herself as a mother, wife, artist, director, photographer and free thinker. Sam directed her first film, *Nowhere Boy*, in 2009, based on the childhood experiences of the Beatles songwriter and singer John Lennon. In 2015 she directed the film adaptation of E. L. James' bestselling novel, *Fifty Shades of Grey* and in 2017 was director and executive producer for the Netflix TV series, *Gypsy*. Sam has battled two life-threatening illnesses during the past twenty years. She learned Transcendental Meditation five years ago.

'My life is always full and I balance a lot. I have four children and I am hopefully raising them to be strong women. I also have a career in a tough industry. I need to mark out time to grant myself stillness in order to step back into the chaos with clarity.

'During a typical filming day, I wake up at 4.30 a.m., half an hour before I need to be up getting ready for work, and I sit for a precious twenty minutes to meditate. Those twenty minutes guide my sanity in an insane working environment; without those twenty minutes I don't think I would cope as well as I do.'

Sam said that going through a major illness was a life changing and immensely challenging experience.

'Even to this day, I sometimes feel a fear that comes out of the dark and threatens to overwhelm me. Practising TM helps me deal with those moments so that the fear doesn't debilitate me. I find that when I practise consistently, my creative thoughts become clearer and, without the interference of all my to-do lists and distractions, I can see where an idea needs to be taken.

'Transcendental Meditation gives me support in all the choices I make. It gives me strength to be bold yet also to be quiet amidst the noise.'

PILLAR *two*

Starting the Process

Let's get to it. The Transcendental Meditation technique is typically taught over four consecutive days, about ninety minutes each day. What happens in each of those sessions? All the information you will need to embark on the next phase of learning to meditate is detailed in this book.

First, after you decide you want to learn (because you read this book and/or attended an introductory talk online or at your local TM centre) but before you take the first step to be taught in personal instruction, you will meet with a TM teacher for a few minutes to ask any questions you might have about the practice. To better prepare the teacher to instruct you, you will also be asked to fill out a simple one-page 'interview' form. The questions are pretty basic.

- What are your reasons for wanting to learn TM?
- What is your overall mood and state of health?
- Do you sleep well at night?
- What previous experience of meditation have you had, if any?

Your answers to these straightforward questions are helpful for your teacher in providing you with personalized instruction.

Also during this initial meeting, your teacher will talk about the tradition of great meditation teachers who have safeguarded the knowledge of transcendence for millennia, and about the traditional way a TM teacher acknowledges this lineage of teachers today. Prior to the instruction, your teacher will perform a simple thank you ceremony – an ancient way of expressing gratitude to the teacher. It's a lovely cultural tradition and not religious in any way. It reminds your teacher to maintain the integrity and accuracy of the steps of instruction to ensure maximum benefit for those who learn in the future. You won't, of course, be asked to participate in it. The thank-you includes a few flowers, some fresh fruit, a candle, a stick of incense, and, to represent the tradition of meditation teachers, a picture of Maharishi's teacher, Guru Dev.

I have instructed many hundreds of devoutly religious

people of all faiths, and when I describe the ceremony, some initially think it could be religious. But when I explain its purpose, they appreciate it. To honour one's teacher like this is rare in our modern world – but not altogether unfamiliar. One cardiologist I taught said it was similar to the Hippocratic oath he took in preparation to becoming a doctor. I instructed a tough-as-nails military officer, and he told me that he found it extremely touching. It reminded him of the honour ceremonies he took part in as a young cadet at his academy. Sometimes students try to read something into the thank you ceremony. One asked me recently to comment on the significance of why white tulips were used that day. 'They looked fresh at the store,' I said with a smile. It's that straightforward.

Once you are satisfied that all of your questions have been answered, you will be escorted to a private room much like a small conference room in a doctor's office. You sit comfortably in a chair across from your teacher. It's a place of calm quiet, with no music or unnecessary trappings.

After your teacher says 'Thank you' to the tradition, he or she will give you your mantra. Its sole purpose is to serve as a vehicle for transcending – one that allows your busy, active mind to settle to its own deepest level, the source of thought.

It's important that the mantra has no meaning associated with it. Why? Because if it meant something, you'd be stuck in the superficial 'gotta-gotta-gotta' level of the mind – trying to explore different avenues of meaning. Then you won't settle down, you won't transcend, you won't meditate. It's also important that the effects of the mantra are known to exert a positive influence. Why? Because any sound, positive or negative, has a powerful influence on the brain and the rest of the nervous system. Remember the sound of fingernails scraping across a chalkboard? Awful. As a TM teacher, I want to be sure that the mantra you are using to meditate will have only positive, life-supporting effects on your mind and body – both on the surface level of thinking but also on the deeper, more powerful levels of the mind. The mantras have been time-tested over thousands of years, and the effects have been documented by hundreds of studies. Both confirm that TM is beneficial and safe. In fact, there has never been any study published in a peer-reviewed journal that has shown any negative impact, only positive.

People I teach naturally ask how I choose the mantra. I liken the selection to that of a medical doctor who has specialized training in how to identify a person's blood type, whether it is, for example, type A, B, or

O. With TM, the selection of the mantra is based on three things: (1) the information you filled out on your interview form, (2) the personal meeting with a TM teacher, and (3) your TM teacher's own comprehensive certification training. All this ensures that you will be given the mantra that is best suited for you – and then, importantly, taught how to use it properly.

Receiving your mantra is only part of the instruction – and takes only a few minutes. The rest of the instruction on day one and the following three days involves learning how to meditate – how to use the mantra properly, without effort, concentration, or control. Some people who hear about TM in a casual way think, 'Just give me the mantra, and I'll figure out how to use it.' That misses the point. The mantra is not like taking a pill. The mantra alone does nothing. You could have the best car in the world, but if you don't know how to drive it, you won't go anywhere. You need both: the car and the training to drive.

A big misconception about the mantra is that you have to repeat it over and over to drive out thoughts. That's not Transcendental Meditation. Here the mantra serves as a vehicle to lead the mind to the source of thought. Learning how to use the mantra properly is a simple but a very individual experience. You are learning how to access the deepest core of your own being.

A teacher works with you, and only you, in the initial session. There is a lot of back-and-forth, a lot of questions and answers, and then you 'get' it. And you will get it, even if you think you will be the only person in the world who won't.

What does it feel like to meditate? Physically, it's very relaxing. Mentally, it's calming yet awakening – and deeply satisfying. Many people tell me they feel that time passes quickly. The adage 'Time flies when you're having a good time' is true. There's usually a double take when they ask how long they'd been meditating. 'It felt like five minutes!' they'll say.

A frequent question is: How do I sit? The answer is: comfortably. As I said earlier, there is no particular way to sit and no specific way to position your hands. Do you need to stretch your legs? Or shift positions in the middle of the meditation? Do it. Nor do you need any special type of chair. In my office, students sit on folding chairs, easy chairs, or a sofa. Just use a chair you like. Whatever is available. Trust me: at one time or another, you'll find yourself meditating in a taxi or on a train or plane. It works fine. I've even meditated at Yankee Stadium. It was an amazing confluence of two loves – meditation and baseball. Noise is no obstacle to transcending.

You will also learn simple best practices that seem

obvious but aren't, such as 'It's best to turn off your mobile phone when you meditate,' and 'Don't meditate right after drinking a double espresso or eating a burrito.' (Note: there's good logic here. Caffeine and digesting a burrito both raise your metabolic rate, and when you meditate, your body wants to rest. *Deeply*. I know. I tried both. That didn't work out so well.)

This one-to-one session with your teacher clarifies the mechanics so that you feel completely comfortable with the practice – and get the absolute maximum out of your twenty-minute meditation. You will leave ready to learn and experience more.

—————————— · ——————————

MEDITATIVE MOMENT
Like Taking Your Mind to a Spa

Donna Rockwell is a Renaissance woman: a clinical psychologist and mindfulness teacher who started her career as a producer and a reporter covering Capitol Hill for the fledgling CNN. She started TM recently as a complement to her twenty-year dogged commitment to practising mindfulness. I was interested in what she thought of both practices, and we talked a few months into her new experience.

When I first got into mindfulness, I went to a teacher who was very involved with Shambhala Meditation. He gave me mindful awareness meditation instructions, and I was supposed to sit there with him for five minutes. Within thirty seconds, I thought my head was going to pop off. I could not do it for the life of me. I saw how type A I was, and I was so disturbed that I had no stillness whatsoever, that I then completely dedicated myself to the practice of meditation.

For me, mindfulness has been a boot camp training of reining in the tendency of the mind to wander. You notice that tendency to wander and, albeit very tenderly, bring the mind back. There's this notion that the mind is a wild horse that is constantly bucking in a very small corral. The goal of mindfulness is to make that corral larger and create a wide-open pasture in which to train the mind to come back to the present moment. After twenty years of practising mindfulness, I am better trained to be in the here and now because of all my hours and hours and weekends and days of just sitting in one spot and looking at a dot on the floor. I am better able to activate my brain's prefrontal cortex and have an awareness that I am having amygdala stimulation.

Now that I've added TM to my practice, it's a completely different thing. While I think mindfulness is 'mind training,' TM is more like taking the mind to an amazing spa. From the very first time, it felt like my brain was settling into a nice warm bath. My brain calms down and my whole system returns to a state of homeostasis, balance.

I think the practices beautifully complement each other. Granted, mindfulness is not twenty minutes. When you go on a mindfulness retreat, you sit for forty minutes, then you walk for ten, more or less, you sit for another forty minutes, you walk for ten, you sit for forty minutes, you get up again – all the while becoming aware of wandering thoughts and coming back to the present moment. Like I said: boot camp.

TM says, 'You've worked so hard all these years to be a more enlightened person. Now here's a meditation practice where you can simply sit for twenty minutes and become naturally refreshed by allowing the mind to settle down.' Yes, you think the mantra but you don't have to strain about it. Your mind goes where it wants to go, towards something more satisfying. Then, after TM's twenty-minute mental spa treatment, I return to my day revitalized and ready for what awaits.

———————— · ————————

Points of Correct Practice

This second day of instruction, and the next two classes as well, usually take place in small groups with others who learned to meditate the day before. It's a time to discuss what you experienced while meditating on your own, either at home or work. It is also valuable for your own practice to talk with others who are learning how to meditate. These sessions are usually held at your local TM centre or, if you are learning as part of a wellness programme at your school or business, on-site there.

This is an opportunity for your teacher to refresh the correct mechanics of TM practice: how not to concentrate or control your mind – something you may have learned from other techniques. The class is also about reassurance. The process is so natural, so effortless, for many people it almost seems too good to be true. It can even raise doubts. One of the first things people say is 'That's great. It's so easy. Could I possibly be doing this right?' Yes, you are. It is that easy.

I remind everyone that every meditation will be different because your body is different each time you sit to meditate. But you will know you are meditating properly in these beginning days if (1) it's easy to do, (2) you feel some deep relaxation during the practice, and (3) you feel a sense of wellbeing afterward. Nothing flashy, but nonetheless, its cumulative impact on your life will be significant.

During this session, your teacher will also talk about the finer points of the practice. You will be encouraged to meditate twice a day. The first meditation is in the morning, before breakfast. This allows the slower brain waves of sleep to shift naturally to the faster, more wakeful, and coherent alpha-1 brain waves of deep meditation. Your morning meditation gives you greater energy and resilience so that you don't take on as much stress during the day.

The second meditation is best done in the late afternoon or early evening, before dinner if possible. You rid your body of much of the stresses that accumulate during the day so that you are better able to be present and available for the people you love in the evening. Plus, you will sleep better at night and wake up feeling fresher in the morning. That said, it's not ideal to meditate right before bed. TM does produce a deep state of rest, but it is also quite energizing. So you may not be able to fall asleep following a late-night meditation.

People ask how they will know when the twenty minutes of the meditation are up. I smile and say, 'Look at your watch!' This is not hypnosis, and you're not in a zone. You are just settling down, physically and mentally, while remaining wide awake inside. Many people find that within a few days of learning TM, the body's internal clock somehow knows exactly when twenty minutes is up, within a minute or so. But whatever you do, please don't set an alarm. It can be incredibly jarring. Plus, you will have to turn it off.

People also ask, 'What if I fall asleep?' I say, 'Good, sleep.' If you fall asleep during meditation, it's healthy, it's revitalizing. It will just be for a minute or two. It's not some superficial catnap – it's a deep rest that helps to heal and rejuvenate the body.

_____ • _____

MEDITATIVE MOMENT
It brings joy, calm and clarity

Shane Anselmi is a self-described 'proud New Zealander'. He is the third generation of Anselmi footwear retailers, and the founder and CEO of the Overland Footwear Group, which has three brands, Overland, Mi Piaci and Merchant 1948, and operates 60 stores in New Zealand and Australia. Overland Footwear has three times been voted New Zealand's 'Best Workplace'. Shane is married with three adult children and lives in Auckland.

I first learned TM in my twenties at my parent's suggestion; they were great role models. TM helped me through challenging times when I built several businesses in my early twenties but then lost them in the 1987 share-market crash. Fortunately, meditation helped me get back on my feet and rebuild. But as success came, for some reason I stopped meditation. It's hard to explain but sometimes you walk away from the thing that helped you the most. Then a couple of years ago things in the fashion industry got really tough and we started going through challenging times. I remembered how TM had helped me cope. I restarted my TM practice, and now for the past eighteen months I have been meditating every day, twice a day, and I love it. It is something

I look forward to because it brings a relaxed peace; a sense of joy, calm and clarity; and allows me to access new levels of creativity. And now, any feeling of anxiety seems to disappear. The other amazing benefit is sleep.

In the past, particularly during busy times, I would often wake between 3 a.m. and 4 a.m. and my mind would start following thoughts or problems, and it was difficult getting back to sleep. Now that I'm meditating I sleep really well. Our business is also back on track – we are thirty times larger than we were when I had stopped meditating. We employ 600 people, mainly millennials, in three countries, and have 60 fashion shoe stores and a factory. I've offered TM training to all our people, and those who have learned love it.

My wife, Louise, and my three adult kids also meditate. Our relationship is better than ever. Louise heads our design department with the pressure of getting the best from our creative team and turning out new, successful ranges on a regular basis. Louise also had severe problems sleeping through the night. Now, after meditating twice a day, she sleeps well and right through the night and experiences many of the benefits I do.

I'm so sold on the benefits of TM that I want to start rolling out the programme in New Zealand schools through our Deuce Sneaker Charity 'The Young Hearts Project.' In this beautiful country, we have one of the highest youth suicide rates in the western world. I've seen the fantastic progress the David Lynch Foundation is making with Transcendental Meditation in schools in the US, and I believe teaching kids here to meditate will make profound differences in their lives. We want New Zealand to be the best country in the world for young people to grow up in.

———————— • ————————

I know a lot of highly competitive men and women who love to proclaim, almost defiantly, 'I love stress. I couldn't live without it.' They have relied on their 'edge' for so long that they don't think they can continue to do their work effectively without it. Yes, they may love negotiating a deal that leaves their client doing a victory lap, but they won't love the tension headache that goes with it. Or the hours of lost sleep because they can't switch off their brain at night. Or the lack of mental space they have to devote to their loved ones.

These problems – some just a nuisance, others signs of something possibly serious developing – can markedly impact your health and performance over time. Meditating does not mean that life's unexpected challenges and obstacles suddenly disappear. It does mean, however, that you will be better equipped to take on those challenges with greater energy, focus and resilience. You can lessen the effects of stress and still have those same victories for yourself and your clients.

Take my friend Rick Goings, who has been the CEO of Tupperware Brands Corporation since 1992. He's a veteran who was a Navy petty officer in the Vietnam era and remains incredibly youthful in his early seventies. Rick is, frankly, the last man you'd peg as passive. And he meditates each and every day. 'I always talk with our people about how you can decide how you're going to approach life,' he said. 'You can either be a warrior or a victim – and, you know, too many people are victims. "Poor me, poor this, poor that."'

Transcendental Meditation, Rick told me, prepares him to conquer those setbacks. 'Bad stuff happens in life,' he said. 'The key word is: responsibility. It isn't a heavy word. It just means owning your ability to respond to situations outside your control. You know how every sport has a ready position? TM keeps me in a ready position for life.'

Another student of mine is Bill Koenigsberg, founder and CEO of Horizon Media, the largest and fastest-growing privately held media services agency in the world. The agency, which he founded in 1989, is consistently recognized as one of the best places to work in the industry, and Bill is the only person to ever win the prestigious Advertising Age Media Maven Award *twice*. He's been making deals since he was fourteen, when he managed tennis courts. (That's where he brainstormed his first ad job, letting a nearby restaurant advertise at the tennis centre in return for free lunches.) He's a great, generous man, *and* he is tremendously busy. And he was one of those people who thought he didn't have time to meditate.

'I was a total sceptic,' he told me. 'Twenty minutes, twice a day, seven days a week, fifty-two weeks a year? Could I actually do that? How on earth do you have the time?'

But he accepted the challenge, carving out time by waking twenty-five minutes earlier than normal. Three years into his practice, 'It's just part of my routine now,' he said. 'I can do it in a car, I can do it on a plane. I close the door for twenty minutes in my office and go do it. And if I don't do it, I feel that I've missed out on something very special.'

That's Bill as an individual, but remember that in business, relationships are everything. Early on in his meditation practice, Horizon's head of human resources told the CEO what an impact TM was making on him. He recalled her saying, 'You're so much calmer, more patient, more present, you're less reactive, and your perspective seems so much more balanced and assertive in a thoughtful way. Your meditation is good for everyone.'

It was a marker of change, he said. 'I didn't even

think of myself as an overly aggressive person, but I guess that says in a nutshell what it did for me in a short period of time.' Bill is so impressed by the results for himself that he plans to offer it to his employees.

For Marilyn Frobuccino, finding the time to meditate is not an option, it is a necessity. As an executive chef, she has run award-winning restaurants in New York and was head chef at the Soho Grand Hotel and at JPMorgan Chase & Co. in Manhattan. Marilyn, who has practised TM for two years, now works as a private chef – an incredibly demanding, time-consuming job. 'When you're a private chef, you make twenty-one different meals each week,' she explained. 'You have to be extremely flexible and deal with other people's changing schedules and dietary needs.'

It's not only demanding but also stressful. 'I always had a low-level anxiety that was job related,' she said. 'Beyond creating menus and competition with other chefs, every day I had to prove myself as a woman in my industry. Whether it was to a general manager, or a new food and beverage rep, or a restaurant manager, there was always that level of stress, anxiety and competition. Since I've been meditating, I feel I manage all of it better. I have to, because I know stress just builds on itself – and if I don't have an outlet, it just accumulates.'

*   *   *

I know the realities of work life. Your day is so packed you eat lunch at your desk or during a meeting. But some of the busiest people I know find ways to get in their twenty minutes in the morning and afternoon. Maybe not always, of course, but most always. For the morning one, they get up twenty minutes earlier. It's more rejuvenating than sleep, so it's not that difficult. (Plus, since they are sleeping better, twenty minutes less sleep is not the end of the world.) For the afternoon, I know a lot of people who schedule it as a regular appointment in their daily calendar, as they would an important meeting. If your office or home is not an ideal place for meditation, you can slip out to a public space, like a park bench or even a church. Remember, you don't have to be in a completely quiet space to meditate. You can do it pretty much anywhere.

It isn't just the demands of work that make people think they won't be able to stick to the twice-a-day regimen. It's the demands of home life as well. Many parents of young children wonder if it's realistic to make time to meditate on a daily basis. Tell mums or dads 'Just get up twenty minutes earlier,' and they roll their eyes and say that their kids will probably just do the same. For some, evenings can be a challenge because parents have been conditioned to make the most of every moment with their kids. I deeply appreciate the difficulties, but meditation is vitally important, and they should do the best they can. When parents take time out to meditate, they are sending a message to their kids that a few minutes of rest and rejuvenation in the midst of an impossibly busy day is not an indulgence but rather an essential component of a healthy, productive lifestyle. You are making meditation a priority in your life – and your kids will carry that lesson with them for the rest of their lives.

Whenever I hear from a parent, 'I just won't have time; my kids won't let me,' I think of Katherine, a single mum I met a few years back.

'I knew I could do my twenty-minute meditation in the morning before the kids wake up,' she told me when she first started. 'But I can't meditate at work, and my bus ride home is too short, so my big concern is what I'll do in the evening once I get home. How am I going to check their homework, fix dinner, talk about their day, be present, *and* meditate? I multitask while brushing my teeth.'

'Call me in two weeks,' I said.

Two weeks went by, and sure enough, Katherine was on the line.

'I'm doing it twice a day,' she said proudly.

'What happened?'

She laughed. 'My kids happened. Now when I get home, and I start snapping at them about homework or dinner, they say, "Mummy, have you meditated?"

Because they know that if they give me the time, they will get "Mum" back – and not the stressed-out Mum, but the more patient, present, loving Mum.'

That's exactly right. It is not narcissistic to meditate, and it is definitely not just 'Leave Mummy alone for twenty minutes.' The children get back a mother who is not carrying frustrations and fatigue from the day. They get an even better parent who is not just going through the motions of being present because it is a checkbox on that laundry list of responsibilities. And they see someone modelling self-care and resilience.

Daisy Lowe is a British fashion model, actress, entrepreneur and television personality. She learned to meditate five years ago, inspired by her godmother Zoe Grace. 'Zoe had a calm in her eyes from her TM practice that I realized I needed in my own life,' Daisy recalls. 'I live a very full life. I am very busy most of the time. But I have always been prone to anxiety, depression and insomnia. When I meditate twice a day, which I always try to do, it helps me stay grounded, eases my anxiety and I sleep much better. It has also been huge for helping me make calm and clear decisions and for centering me through the chaos of my working life,' Daisy says. Interestingly, for such a highly public woman, she says that she isn't as fearful of public speaking. 'I used to shake like a leaf in the storm and stutter over most words. But after learning to meditate I was pleasantly surprised that in fact I was as cool as a cucumber! TM has really improved my life in so many ways.'

(Daisy is working with the David Lynch Foundation to bring Transcendental Meditation to women and children in the UK who are survivors of domestic violence and sexual assault.)

The world is as you are. If you are stressed, wound tight, exhausted, consumed by worry, then *all* of your relationships at work and home are going to be affected – meaning more contentiousness and less satisfaction. But if you are strong and connected within yourself, and you naturally have a lot to give, you won't be expecting a partner or child to make you happy all the time. You won't come home or go to work with a chip on your shoulder. You won't enter a negotiation with your amygdala doing the thinking, itching for a fight. You will make decisions with a healthy brain.

Maharishi put it this way:

> If the individual has fully developed potential, he'll enjoy friendships, relationships and marriage to the fullest extent ... Therefore the key to relationships is to take care of our own Self. We meditate, and then

our potentiality is being used more and more through practice, and then a time will come when we are using our full potential, and we have a fully developed heart and mind. And with a fully developed heart and mind, all relationships will be enjoyed just because we are able to give maximum of ourselves to others.

---------------- • ----------------

MEDITATIVE MOMENT
Time with Your True Self

I first met the incredibly talented Hugh Jackman, and his equally extraordinary wife, Deborra-lee Furness, when I taught TM to their son, Oscar, who showed an interest in meditation at a young age. I actually started calling him Oscar Yogi because he is just preternaturally wise. As a twelve-year-old, he and I would have long conversations about anthropology, history, religion, philosophy – it was hard for me to keep up.

Hugh had learned to meditate while in drama school in Australia, but he and Deborra-lee 'relearned' with me. 'I'm of the school that you should always be ready to learn something,' Hugh told me. 'TM has really helped.'

I'm someone who is diligent and disciplined. A lot of people get stuck on the idea of meditating twice a day. I didn't get stuck on that, but there was this little bit of a shadow of a thought of 'This is good for me. I should do this. I've *got* to meditate' – which is exactly the thing you're trying to get away from in meditation. That 'gotta' mind. 'I've *got* to meditate. I've *got* to wake up so I can meditate.' So when I learned with Bob, that completely went away. That idea of giving myself a hard time about it, stressing if I fell asleep or if my mind was going nonstop – all those judgements about it really went away.

There is a level of stress to my job that is easy to buy into. You don't necessarily know what is coming up next month or next year. It doesn't matter how long you're doing it, each new role or new job you do, whether it's hosting or an acting role or film or theatre, there's some element about it that is risky, that is frightening and that can bring stress. It's also a good thing because, creatively, it's healthy to have a sense of the unknown as I try something I haven't done before. It kind of brings things out of yourself that surprise you. But I used to find that stress difficult to cope with. I would internalize it. My wife used to say, after I completed something I was nervous about, 'Oh good, I got my husband back.' I was not fully there because a part of my brain – a big part or a small part, depending on the job – was concentrating on what was going to happen. For me, the best way to handle that has been meditation.

So, of course, I meditated before I hosted the Oscars.

I meditate before I go onstage. I meditate in the morning and lunchtime when I'm on a film set. It's like a reset. I'm not saying I'm never frightened anymore or that I don't have stress, but I like the analogy of a glass of water. When you first pour it, it's cloudy. When you're stressed, that's what your mind is like: it's kind of cloudy. And after I meditate, all that sinks to the bottom, and the water is clear, and the energy is finer, and the decisions you make are more authentic. I think you're more economical with your energy, with your time, in every way. You're more able to listen to other people, and, as an actor, that's what you've got. The only tools I really have are being present, being clear and listening.

When I meditate, I'm joining my true self, which is this calm, peaceful, blissful, limitless self. I can then parlay that into any situation. When I walk out of a car on a red carpet and there's three thousand people cheering, deep down, actually I'm connecting with their calm inner self. It's not that I don't get excited or that you don't enjoy life or I don't go crazy sometimes. I have fun, but there's always one thought a little outside going, 'This is fun, but really it's all calm,' and that's how meditation has helped. It doesn't matter what situation I'm in. People say, 'Oh, you're down-to-earth.' No, it's just that meditation makes me see what's true and real.

————————— • —————————

DAY THREE

Success Without Stress

On this third day of instruction, I talk about the impact of stress on life and the mechanics of how the TM technique helps to neutralize its buildup.

Believe it or not, stress has not always been the enemy. I know that statement might sound ridiculous given what I have said about the dangers of stress. But for much of our two-hundred-thousand-year human history, our stress response system was one of the body's most important survival tools.

Let's jump back to when your ancestors were hunters having a normal day in the savannas of Africa. They'd be walking along and suddenly find themselves eye-to-eye with a lion. Without conscious thought, they either dug in their heels and gripped their spears, or they turned and ran for their sweet lives.

That is why we still have what's called the fight-or-flight response. Back then, if you saw a lion or heard the roar, that information went to your amygdala, the little almond-shaped set of nerve cells (neurons) deep in your brain. The amygdala is the fire alarm that tells your body it's under attack. When any human is under stress, two hormones – the chemical messengers cortisol and epinephrine (also known as adrenaline) – flood the bloodstream in a lightning-quick process.

Today, if we are already in a high state of stress and anxiety, 'the lion on the savanna' can be a child throwing a temper tantrum right before school, a major traffic jam blocking your way to a critical meeting, a high-stakes exam for a maths class tomorrow morning, or an elderly parent suffering from late-stage Alzheimer's disease. When you have experiences like that, often repeatedly, you might shorthand it as 'I'm really stressed.'

It's hard to know what will set us off. I know a woman who is a principal soloist with one of the world's most celebrated opera companies. I mentioned to her that performing before thousands of people in a grand concert hall night after night must be incredibly stressful. She said, 'Oh, that's easy. It's the train ride getting to the concert hall that stresses me out!'

Life is filled with inevitable external demands, challenges, illnesses and so on. Science calls these stressors: financial stressors, family stressors, job stressors, social stressors. You can try to manage or minimize stressors, but the truth is that they will always be there. And these days, it seems we have little or no control over most of them.

The real issue is how we *react* to those stressors. This is what scientists call our stress response. If we are well rested, thinking clearly, and on top of our game, we meet these stressors head-on. Afterwards, we feel good, invigorated, satisfied, ready for the next challenge. But if we are not sleeping well, not thinking particularly clearly, and feeling off, we get overwhelmed. We get *stressed*.

According to research, stress hits us in at least three distinct, often debilitating ways. On the muscular or structural level, we become tense. Tension affects different people in different ways. Some develop tension headaches and a stiff neck and shoulders; or their jaw tightens up, and they grind their teeth at night; or their stomach knots up; or they get back pain; or their blood vessels constrict, which means less oxygen reaches the brain or heart, increasing the likelihood of a stroke or heart attack. The list goes on.

Second, on the level of cognitive functioning,

reduced circulation to the brain skews its electrical activity, taking key parts of the brain offline. In particular, stress can shut down the *prefrontal cortex*, which functions as the brain's CEO. The prefrontal cortex is about the size of your fist and sits right behind your forehead. It takes in all the information (motor, sensory, and so forth) from the outside world transmitted to it from the other areas of the brain and helps you decide your next moves. The prefrontal cortex governs executive functioning: judgement, problem solving, ethical reasoning and your sense of self. (Side note: The prefrontal cortex is not integrated with the rest of the brain in a teenager. In fact the connections between the prefrontal cortex and the rest of the brain are not completed until the middle or late twenties, often even later in life. That's why teenagers frequently don't consider the consequences of risky behaviours.)

With the CEO offline, the amygdala takes over the command of the brain. That's a good thing if a lion is about to attack you, because the amygdala is the fight-or-flight, or 'emergency,' centre of the brain. But it's not good if your amygdala goes ballistic while you are stuck in traffic.

If the prefrontal cortex is the calm, rational, creative, insightful CEO, your amygdala is the hyperreactive, paid-by-the-hour security guard, itching for a fight. It deals only with crises, with an impending attack, with the most urgent matters at hand. It's a 'yes' to instantaneous reactions; to punch and counterpunch. It's a 'no' to long-term planning, seeing the big picture and pausing to reflect. Foresight and compassion are not in the amygdala's job description.

With chronic stress, you're chronically acting from that fear centre. Do you make good decisions when you're stressed? Display sound judgement? Solve problems? Plan well? Of course not. With a hyperaroused amygdala, you overreact to just about everything. You don't think as clearly, your memory is less reliable, you can get sick more often, and you just don't feel 'yourself.'

The third component is that our stress response stimulates the adrenal gland atop each kidney to secrete too much cortisol, now popularly known as the stress hormone. This feeds anxiety, and then the adrenals pump out more cortisol, which makes us even more anxious. Stress has turned our bodies into walking cortisol factories. Elevated cortisol destroys healthy muscle and bone; slows healing and normal cell regeneration; co-opts biochemicals needed to make other vital hormones; impairs digestion, metabolism and mental function; and weakens the immune system. It also affects your most basic functions, such as memory. It's why you can't remember people's names at a job interview. Or why you check the address for a date three times. Cortisol also stimulates your appetite, which, of course, increases your weight. Finally, it has an adverse effect on your sleep. Cortisol suppresses your body's production of the hormone melatonin, which is integral to your sleep cycle. Troubled sleep can be the real killer.

Organizational psychologist Cary Cooper, a leading authority on workplace stress, opined in an interview that stress is the black plague of the twenty-first century. For many people, modern medicine offers little to prevent stress and often has nothing to cure it.

Norman Rosenthal is a Georgetown University School of Medicine clinical professor of psychiatry, a medical researcher, and the author of the books *Winter Blues: Everything You Need to Know to Beat Seasonal Affective Disorder* and *Super Mind: How to Boost Performance and Live a Richer and Happier Life Through Transcendental Meditation*. As a senior researcher for twenty years at the National Institute of Mental Health, Dr Rosenthal was the first to describe seasonal affective disorder (SAD) and prescribe light therapy as a treatment. Dr Rosenthal has been practising TM for eight years, and in his private practice he sees people from all walks of life who come to him with many different concerns. But one theme that runs through all of their worries is stress – its impact on their lives and their struggle to find ways to deal with it more effectively.

'After discovering the value of TM to me personally,' Dr Rosenthal explained, 'I began to recommend it to my patients and clients, many of whom now practise it regularly. In almost forty years as a psychiatrist, Transcendental Meditation stands out as one of the most powerful and effective techniques I have encountered for reducing stress.'

I want to shift gears here and take a moment to talk in some detail about some of the truly breakthrough research documenting the unique and profound benefits TM has on stress and health.

It's common knowledge that two of the biggest killers in developed countries are heart attack (myocardial infarction) and stroke – two conditions that are often the direct result of damaged arteries from stress. Arteries are the pipes that carry oxygenated blood pumped by the heart to all the tissues in our bodies. When their linings are damaged or blocked – as occurs in a condition called atherosclerosis – blood cannot get through in adequate amounts. And then you're talking about a heart attack or stroke, which will either disable you or end your life.

In addition, when stress occurs continuously, blood pressure levels become elevated even at rest. And because there are often no warning symptoms associated with raised blood pressure, the condition has aptly been called 'the silent killer.' In the United States, according to the Centers for Disease Control and Prevention (CDC), seventy-five million adults suffer from hypertension. That's nearly one in three Americans. Cardiovascular disease is the leading cause of death in the United States.[1]

There are many millions of lives at stake here. Could there be potential cardiovascular benefits to TM? One of the first to connect the dots among TM, blood pressure and cardiovascular disease was Dr Robert Schneider, a clinical specialist in hypertension, a fellow of the American College of Cardiology and director of the Institute of Natural Medicine and Prevention at Maharishi University of Management, in Fairfield, Iowa. With $26 million in research grants from the National Institutes of Health (NIH) and elsewhere, Dr Schneider and his team conducted randomized, controlled studies to investigate the effect of TM versus health education. The results were clear: Transcendental Meditation reduced blood pressure in as little as three months. [2]

Other investigators went on to replicate Dr

Schneider's findings, leading to an impressive body of research. Dr Jim Anderson and colleagues from the University of Kentucky analyzed data from more than one hundred TM blood pressure studies involving hundreds of people. Blood pressure changes for those in the TM groups included average reductions of five points on systolic blood pressure and 2.8 on diastolic blood pressure. Their overall conclusion was that blood pressure dropped in all groups practising TM compared with the control groups using relaxation, stress management and biofeedback.[3]

However, for Dr Schneider and others, a question remained: Would the short-term benefits on blood pressure also produce long-term gains? To discover the answer, he received a research grant from the NIH to analyze the death records of 202 of the participants in his initial TM and blood pressure randomized trials, to see if they were healthy and still alive. In 2005 Dr Schneider's team struck gold, finding a 23 per cent reduction in the death rate among those who had been assigned to the TM group ten years before as compared with those who'd received only health education. On top of that, there was a 30 per cent reduction in the death rate from cardiovascular causes.[4]

Dr Schneider then received funding for a clinical trial to compare TM with health education. Once again, TM proved superior. Keep in mind that these people were already ill at the start of the study and were already undergoing standard care, such as medications for hypertension and high cholesterol, and advice about diet and exercise. These standard-of-care treatments continued throughout the study. After five years, the group doing TM fared much better than the group doing health education. In fact, the TM group had a 48 per cent reduction in the risk of dying from myocardial infarction and stroke, as well as from *all causes*.[5]

In 2013 the American Heart Association looked at the years of research on TM and concluded in its journal *Hypertension* that TM is the only meditation technique shown to lower blood pressure.[6]

Besides helping people live longer, there is compelling evidence that TM can help young people who are highly stressed to live better by alleviating high blood pressure. Vernon A. Barnes, a physiologist at the Medical College of Georgia, set out to examine the impact of TM on cardiac and blood pressure reactivity (response to stress) in thirty-five volunteers ages fifteen to eighteen with high–normal blood pressure. Dr Barnes divided his subjects into two groups: the experimental group practised TM twice a day for two months, while the control group received weekly one-hour health education lectures over the same period of time.

To make the study as true to life as possible, Dr Barnes also monitored changes in blood pressure, heart rate and cardiac output in the teens as they underwent interviews about emotionally charged subjects. He also recorded the teens' same cardiovascular reactivity as he or she 'drove' in a virtual-reality driving programme with built-in stressors. Whether the young people were handling tough topics or troubleshooting obstacles on 'the road,' Dr Barnes's research revealed that those who practised TM maintained lower blood pressure than the control group members did. Not only that, but the TM group's blood pressure readings remained lower during periods of rest.[7]

Finally, two studies have tested whether TM meditators and nonmeditators respond differently to stress by placing two electrodes on their skin to measure their galvanic skin response (GSR). When you feel anxious, you sweat more, which increases the electrical current transmitted between the electrodes. This is indicated by an upward blip on a graph. Conversely, when you relax, the current decreases, resulting in a corresponding downward blip. (GSR is a major component of a lie detector test, or polygraph.)

In one of these TM studies evaluating galvanic skin response, psychologist David Orme-Johnson exposed fourteen meditators and sixteen nonmeditators to unpleasantly loud noises and compared their GSR responses. In all subjects, the GSR showed an upward blip, but the meditators demonstrated a quicker return to baseline levels. The nonmeditators not only returned to baseline more slowly but also had more 'false alarms': further upward blips even when the irritating noise was no longer present. In the other study, this one by researchers Daniel Goleman and Gary Schwartz at Harvard University, the stressful stimuli were scenes of horrible injuries from an occupational safety movie, which meditators and nonmeditators were asked to watch. Once again, the meditators' GSRs returned more rapidly to baseline levels.

Finally, to return to the pressing issue of high cortisol levels and health, a number of studies have found reduced blood cortisol levels both during TM and post-TM. In one clinical trial, for example, people who had meditated for an average of three to five years showed a statistically significant 30 per cent drop in their circulating cortisol levels during meditation, as compared with controls. Those who had been meditating for three to four months showed a trend in the same direction, though it did not reach significance. In another study, subjects who had been practising TM for a relatively short four-month duration had lower cortisol levels than controls when they were *not* meditating – both at rest and when subjected to stresses such as mental arithmetic or squeezing on an isometric hand grip.

According to Dr Norman Rosenthal, 'The bottom line is that no matter how you measure it, the practice of TM has powerful and sustained beneficial effects on how we deal with stress, which are significant not only in the laboratory but in the real world, leading to substantial reductions in serious diseases and increased longevity.'

Jerry Seinfeld told me he's felt the effects of deep rest so profoundly that he likens TM to a phone charger for the mind. 'The phone charger is pretty tough to beat as an analogy because your phone charger never doesn't work, unless sometimes you haven't got it all the way in the outlet, you know?' he said. 'You look at it and say, "How come it didn't charge?" It's always a little ways out of the outlet, and you go, "Oh, I didn't push it all the way in." And it always works.'

That's the great thing about TM, he continued. 'You never have to wonder. Let's say you've got a big day and the night before you say, "I'm going to get to sleep early. I'm not going to mess around and watch junk TV. I want to get a good night's sleep." But you're still just kind of hoping. You're hoping that you're going to get to sleep and wake up feeling refreshed. And that's the big difference between sleep and TM: TM never doesn't work perfectly.'

I agree with Jerry, but I have to add that *perfectly* is a tricky word. After you have been practising TM for even a few days, you will notice that every meditation is different. It's not rigid like the perfect tennis swing or the perfect chord played on a piano. The experience of transcending is fluid, and every session is influenced by the condition of the body at the time you meditate. I like to say that there is no single perfect experience in meditation – there are countless perfect experiences. People sometimes worry that they didn't have the 'best' meditation session. When asked about this, Maharishi used to say, 'Even in a shallow dive, you still get wet.'

—————— . ——————

MEDITATIVE MOMENT
Better Parents and Better Neighbours

G. Sequane Lawrence is president of Fathers, Families and Healthy Communities (FFHC) in Chicago. His life's mission is to improve the outcomes of children of non-custodial African American dads, by giving those dads tools to heal broken relationships and live healthier lives. He learned to meditate through the David Lynch Foundation, and now he is working to make TM a pillar in their work.

I work with young men who live in some really distressed communities. I don't want to speak with a broad brush, but some of them have seen real trauma. In the community we serve, there can be as many as 50 per cent of the young men with a record. This is a real problem, and it's a consequence of the war on drugs, mass incarceration, racism and all these things I fight against. A lot of them are minors who were then incarcerated with adults. These are young men who want to be better fathers, but one of the issues is the social construct that to be a 'real man' you've got to be a provider, and if you don't do that, your masculinity and manhood are called into question. This causes all kinds of psychological and emotional problems. I tell these young men that you may not have money right now, but you can be a man by the things you learn and then communicate to your kids. I feel they transmit a sense of calm and emotional maturity to their children as a result of their TM practice. I tell them it's a way you can assert yourself as a man in the family, and bring real value and be an asset. TM also helps to remove the rancour that is often there between these young men and the mothers of their children. They become better parents and better neighbours.

My goal is to make TM a fundamental part of our wellness platform in the same way that nutrition, exercise and education are. I also want TM in all of the schools across the district as well as in after-school programmes, community centres, and churches. I think Chicago is ready for it. It might sound strange to some people, but so did jogging and eating organic. They're not fads now.

My wife, Theresa, says she can tell when I am meditating consistently. She likes that man when I'm doing it. We've been married thirty-six years – so this is a person who knows.

_____ • _____

DAY FOUR

Growing the Benefits

Here's the key point I make on the fourth day: you don't meditate for the sake of meditation. It's not an escape. You meditate for the sake of your life. As restful and rejuvenating, as centering and expansive as the experience may be, I always emphasize that what's really important is how you feel afterwards. During this final class of the first four days, we look at the cumulative effects that follow your morning and afternoon practices. And while it's true that you cannot predict what any one particular meditation session may be like because your body is different each time you meditate (for example, Did you sleep well the night before? Eat a big meal right before meditation? Pull an all-nighter studying for an exam?), it's also true that you have every right to assume that if you meditate regularly over time, there will be real, discernible improvements in your life.

How long does it take for such improvements to show up?

It differs for different people. I have taught veterans with post-traumatic stress who have not slept more than one or two hours a night for several months because of terrible nightmares and sweats, but after their first or second day of meditating, they went home and slept through the night. Weeks later, they reported that sleeping through the night has become a new normal. My own experiences when I first learned to meditate were far less dramatic. I mean, I was a stressed-out college kid, not a traumatized war veteran. But within a few weeks, my mind was much clearer, my memory much sharper (a boon for studying), and I was sleeping much better at night. And my experiences have continued to deepen, and the benefits have continued to grow immeasurably over the nearly fifty years that I have continued to meditate.

Studies investigating the effects of TM on cognitive functioning, heart disease, or depression typically last a minimum of eight to twelve weeks. For example, the researchers want to see if a significant drop in high blood pressure or improved mood after one week of meditating is not a coincidence of that particular day but rather a sign of a sustained trend over time. I always suggest this to my students: resolve to meditate for two or three months as prescribed before evaluating if it is valuable. But give it that time.

To explain the cumulative effects of twice-daily meditation, Maharishi often used the analogy of how people in centuries past used to dye a white cloth yellow. First you dip the cloth into a vat of bright yellow dye for a few minutes. Once the colour is fully absorbed, you set the wet cloth out in the sun for many hours to dry. In the process, however, much of the bright yellow colour naturally fades. Nonetheless, a hint of the bright yellow remains colourfast. Again you dip the cloth in the yellow dye for a few minutes and then let it dry in the sun for several hours. A bit more of the yellow is colourfast in the cloth. You repeat over and over again, every day, and there comes a time when the dried cloth in the sun is the same yellow colour as the dye in the vat.

The analogy to the impact of meditation on the mind is simple. Settle down into the field of stillness for a few minutes during your morning meditation and then plunge into dynamic activity. Get the kids off to school, head to work, study for an exam – whatever you ordinarily do. In those beginning days, you may notice that the equanimity and clarity of thinking you feel immediately after your meditation lasts for an hour before it dissipates. Now do that twice a day every day for a week or two – a few minutes of meditation followed by many hours of life – and see for yourself how the inner stillness grows and begins to extend longer and longer throughout your day. Then watch that happen as weeks turn into months and years of regular meditating twice a day.

I want to emphasize that TM is not like blood pressure medication, where your level goes down after you take a pill and then climbs back up over time until you take another one. That's obviously helpful, and very necessary, for people with hypertension, but it doesn't address the underlying issue of how people's bodies react to stress. It's masking or merely managing the problem. In contrast, the research shows that the benefits of TM are cumulative. Not only will your high blood pressure decrease, but a lot of other good, healthy effects will follow. You will be more resilient, efficient and energized, and feel healthier over time. It's not positive thinking; it's not too good to be true. It's simply what happens when you are not tied up in huge knots of stress.

Ray Dalio is the founder, co-chief investment officer, and co-chairman of Bridgewater Associates, a global leader in institutional portfolio management and the largest hedge fund in the world. *Fortune* magazine called Bridgewater the fifth most important private company in the United States. Ray is also the bestselling author of *Principles: Life and Work*.

Ray has been practising Transcendental Meditation for nearly fifty years and calls it 'the single most important reason for any success I have had in my life, because it has given me equanimity and creativity.'

Ray is in his mid-sixties, but he still has the same energy he had as a kid growing up in Queens, New York, with a jazz musician father and a homemaker mum. 'Meditation leads to open-mindedness and creativity,' he said. 'Meditation is a process of opening up. It's like taking a hot shower but better; even though you're not thinking of anything in particular, a great idea can come through, and then you just grab it.

'It also doesn't lessen your emotions. The emotions are the same, but you can step back and say, "I'm not going to be controlled by that emotion." And I think it does help to see things at a higher level,' he said.

I thought about the practical nature of Ray's words about not being controlled by emotions a few weeks later when I was teaching a writer friend who has two boys, ages two and five. He had his very first meditation session with me on a Sunday morning at my Midtown Manhattan office. That night, at bath time, he had trouble convincing his five-year-old to get in the tub. But he stayed calm, and the child didn't get the hoped-for reaction from his dad. 'I was feeling very present,' he said, 'and then my son emptied a bucket of water on me.'

That would usually be just the thing, he admitted, to make him lose his temper. 'But I had a real moment, completely soaked, where I saw the options. I could lose it, yell at him, and make him cry, so he doesn't hear anything I say anyway. Or I could acknowledge the absurdity of it and still be firm about the rules. How many times have I wasted opportunities to help him learn because I reacted purely out of frustration?'

This is the prefrontal cortex of the brain coming back online from daily meditation. It brings broader perspective and gives you a pause, a moment, between the burning feeling of irritation and then lashing out, perhaps irrationally and regretfully.

Dr Fred Travis, director of the Center for Brain, Consciousness and Cognition at Maharishi University of Management, is one of the world's foremost research scientists on meditation and the brain. Even before he became a neuroscientist, Dr Travis wrote his senior thesis at Cornell University on the effect of Transcendental Meditation on creativity. He took a matched group of Cornell undergraduates, some of whom were learning TM and some who were not.

'I would grade all the creativity tests, not knowing who were the meditators and who were not,' he told me. 'I would see huge transitions in some students, and I wondered, "Are these the meditators? They're really seeing things differently and being more creative in their responses." And when we broke the code, they did, in fact, turn out to be in the TM group.'

Later, Dr Travis set out to study how TM could optimize performance and self-development. He used a composite index he developed called the Brain Integration Scale (BIS). The BIS is a combination of three EEG-derived brain measures recorded during challenging tasks: broadband frontal coherence, alpha waves and brain preparatory response. He combined these 'scores' into the BIS, with higher scores relating to creativity, decision making and brain processing speed. When he measured the brain waves of thirty-eight college students, Dr Travis saw the BIS scores rose during three months of TM practice.[8]

Dr Travis hypothesized that elite athletes and top business managers would have similar brain coherence with the various parts of the brain connecting to work together. He tested the brain wave patterns of thirty-three world-class athletes, comparing them to patterns in thirty-three average performing athletes (all matched by age and gender). He measured galvanic skin response, and also gave them paper-and-pencil tests to measure self-development, moral development and frequency of peak experiences – the feeling of being in the zone – during optimum performance. Sure enough, he found that higher psychophysiological growth – a greater sense of wellbeing during action – underlies higher performance.[9] He also compared the brain waves of twenty top-level managers and twenty low-level managers, matched for age, gender, education and type of organization. Top-level managers were characterized by higher BIS scores, higher levels of moral reasoning and more frequent optimum-performance peak experiences.[10]

The evidence is clear: when the different areas of your brain are connected and functioning coherently, you get more done.

But a prefrontal cortex is only as strong as the brain's circuits. The brain is a living organ that adapts to our every experience. The old theory was that the brain grew until the end of adolescence and then remained static – 'as is' – for the rest of your life. Now we know that the brain has neuroplasticity – the ongoing strengthening and weakening of brain circuits – throughout life. Each experience creates electrical activity that travels through the brain's circuits. Trauma and stress generate dysfunctional circuits, while positive experiences produce functional circuits. With each new positive experience, we change brain connections in ways that will allow us to be better at what we do the next time.

Research shows that the experience of inner stillness over time is a healthy, positive one, and it reshapes and strengthens brain connections.

What exactly happens to the brain when you meditate? As I said before, researchers can track its effects by giving the TM practitioner an electroencephalogram (EEG), which measures electrical activity in your brain. When you run an EEG on someone practising TM, you see an increase in alpha-1 brain waves in the prefrontal cortex, and these waves then spread throughout the brain. Alpha-1 waves are the bridge between conscious thinking and our subconscious mind. Another unique characteristic is that these alpha-1 brain waves are coherent: that is, the frequency of brain waves from one point of the brain are similar to those from another point. This coherence is found between the prefrontal cortex and the back of the brain, and between the left and right hemispheres of the brain. Alpha-1 EEG coherence means that different parts of the brain are working together in full communication. What's important here is that this coherence extends far beyond the twenty-minute meditation to enhance your brain function while you are focused on your work during the hours after meditation. (According to a review of the effects of different methods, including Open Monitoring and Focused

Attention, more than a dozen studies reported that TM is the only meditation technique to increase alpha-1 EEG coherence.[11])

These coherent circuits are strengthened as you continue to meditate over days and weeks and months, allowing your brain to work more efficiently and effectively. TM does this in the same way that the neural connections formed during any repeated experience, such as musical training – for example, learning to play the guitar – also prime the brain for other aspects of human communication, like language, speech and memory. But during TM, those connections are unique and have a more holistic impact on brain functioning compared with when you learn to play an instrument or listen to music.

As a result, as you continue to meditate, you increasingly make better decisions with better judgement and planning. You're more yourself. Of course, none of this is magic. It's the way your brain works when all the areas of the brain are connected, integrated and healthy. Dr Travis likens this TM benefit to an orchestra finally playing together in concert. And this is an ongoing process that starts from your first meditation and continues throughout your life.

* * *

David Lynch is a close friend, a brilliant filmmaker (*The Elephant Man*, *Blue Velvet*, *Mulholland Drive*, *Inland Empire*, and many others), and the writer and director of the iconic television show *Twin Peaks*. He is also the founder of the nonprofit in his name, the David Lynch Foundation, which has helped to bring TM to more than six hundred thousand inner-city school kids. David has been meditating since 1973, and he has not missed a single meditation in all that time. For him, the effects of meditating are like 'expanding the container' of his mind. 'The conduit for that flow of ideas is more open,' he told me, 'and you can just start desiring ideas, and they seem to float in.'

As you meditate, you are able to access deeper levels of thought, down to the level of your intuition. 'It's the thing that every artist is looking for,' David explained to me, 'to get the thing that feels correct to us. I say intuition is our number one tool. Intuition is emotion and intellect swimming together. It's something that grows the more you transcend.'

And regular meditation allows you to draw upon your creative resources on a regular basis.

At first, though, David wasn't so sure. 'You hear about meditation and think you're going to get calm, super boring, and you're going to lose your edge,' he said. 'I had that same fear. I thought maybe meditation would make everybody the same, and then they'll ring a bell, and we'll all be out marching somewhere. I was worried about those things.'

Instead, David found that TM gave him more of an edge to do his art and freed him from what he calls 'the suffocating rubber clown suit of negativity.' In his view, anger – real selfish, bitter anger – is nothing less than mind control. 'That anger's controlling you,' he explained. 'It doesn't serve anything. If you're super angry, that just occupies the mind, and there is very little room for ideas to flow in.'

Simply put, chronic stress and fatigue can make everyone look and act pretty much the same – and that means reactive, unhappy, irritable, sick. On the other hand, meditation helps people actualize their own unique potential without being limited or shrouded by stress and fatigue. And that means being more creative, more productive, more fulfilled.

I liken it to an orchard. If you have ten different types of fruit trees, and they haven't been watered for a long time, you will see a landscape of leafless, brittle, brown branches and sticks and stems. But if you water and nourish the trees at their roots, you will see a rich vista of differences. The apple, orange and cherry trees will each be healthy, robust and distinctively themselves, with each one yielding different fragrant flowers and sweet fruits. TM is like watering the roots of your life – it allows you to simultaneously nourish all the different parts of your life, it allows you to be more of who you naturally are.

As this growth continues naturally over time, you will develop the expanded mental faculties that Maharishi and the ancient meditation texts call 'cosmic consciousness' and that Dr Norman Rosenthal calls the 'super mind' in his bestselling book by that title. As Dr Rosenthal puts it: 'The super mind is a mental state that consists of the development of expanded states of consciousness that occur in tandem with reduced stress, better physical health and the emergence of life-enhancing personal qualities.'

Dr Rosenthal emphasizes that as you meditate over time, you don't just become more relaxed and smarter, but also you gain a scarce commodity these days: you actually feel *happier*. He surveyed more than six hundred TM practitioners, a large majority of whom reported that, since starting to meditate, 'they felt as though they had become more mindful, recovered more quickly from unpleasant events, were more fully present and engaged, and were generally happier,' Dr Rosenthal told me. 'They also reported that they felt more in the zone, which was associated with greater ease at getting things done, and improved creativity and productivity. Unsurprisingly, these traits were associated with improved performance at work.'

Those who responded to Dr Rosenthal's question-naire also reported feeling 'luckier,' as though they were receiving more support from those around them. They were making healthier choices in their lives, others noticed their positive changes, and their relationships in general improved. The data also showed that favourable life changes that started after learning to meditate corre-lated significantly with both how long and how regularly people had been meditating.

Finding the time to meditate was the foremost concern of Scott Miller when he walked into my Midtown Manhattan office a little more than four years ago. He had been thinking about learning to meditate for a long time, but the biggest challenge had been making time in his schedule for instruction. It's true – he was indeed very busy. Scott heads up G100 Network, an invitation-only membership organization that brings together current and rising CEOs from around the world to share ideas on leadership and strategy.

Scott, who was CEO of both Hyatt Hotels

Corporation and United Infrastructure Company, has trained and advised hundreds of CEOs and thousands of potential CEOs through G100. He told me he has learned that everyone is a leader in one way or another. But the demands placed on any leader – whether a corporate CEO, teacher, parent, or student – are escalating far beyond the available hours in a day. So having the clarity and scope to prioritize is becoming more and more essential.

A big part of Scott's work nowadays is arming these leaders with tools to help them manage not just their professional lives but also their personal lives. He says that many leaders need to be taught to achieve balance in their lives. Once he learned TM, he knew the technique would be a major tool in that arsenal.

Successful people, he said, want more from life than just high marks in their career. They want to be present and available to their loved ones and fulfilled outside of work. He urges his clients to meditate because he knows it will make them perform better at whatever it is they care about. If their focus is on business, they'll see advancement there. If it's about being a more active father or wife, they will have breakthroughs there. And he finds that when he encounters these leaders after they have been practising even for a few weeks, the difference is remarkable.

'Every single one of them is more resilient,' Scott told me. 'They can balance stresses at work and home so much better.'

One last point here to those who are concerned that they won't be able to meditate twice a day every day. Life intrudes, and, realistically, you're probably going to miss a session. But for your own sake, make that the exception, not the rule. Make it a priority. Of course, I think you should try to do it twice a day, because that is how you will get the most benefit.

Let's review the steps of instruction:

Day 1. Learn to meditate with a certified TM teacher – just you and your teacher (ninety minutes).

Day 2. Establish correct practice of the TM technique so that when you meditate, it is simple, natural and effortless – with no concentration or control of the mind. This is a class with the people who learned to meditate in personal instruction the day before (ninety minutes).

Day 3. Understand the mechanics of how the unique state of restful alertness gained during TM practice allows the body to dissolve deeply rooted stress. This is a class with the same people from the day before (ninety minutes).

Day 4. Gain a vision of possibilities of how the benefits of regular TM practice to mind and body accumulate over time. This is a class with the same people from the previous two days (ninety minutes).

After You Learn. Once you complete the four days of instruction, you have the option to schedule periodic 'refreshers' with your TM teacher (or any TM teacher anywhere in the world) for the rest of your life. These sessions usually take about thirty minutes and are a simple and valuable way to ensure that you are meditating 100 per cent correctly and gaining maximum benefit.

And one last note. Life happens. There will be events in your life that you might need a little support to get through. As TM teachers, we are here for you. And even if you are on a sustained roll, it's nice to have check-in sessions to refresh your practice, to make sure you are on the right track. I just meditated with someone I'd taught in 1972!

He was doing fine. He just wanted to say hello.

———————————— • ————————————

MEDITATIVE MOMENT
From Gang Member to University

When Maria entered New Village Girls Academy in Los Angeles as a fifteen-year-old, she was perceived as having very little chance at succeeding in life. But she learned to meditate through a David Lynch Foundation programme that offered TM to faculty and students at the school. In a pretty dramatic fashion, Maria turned around her life. Right away, she said, she was able to focus better, retain more information, and stay away from drugs and gangs and other bad influences. She began taking advanced classes the next year, along with her required high school subjects. By the middle of her last year in school before college, she was ready to graduate among the top of her class. Maria was admitted to several colleges with her pick of full-paying scholarships.

Maria's story is so compelling that she was asked recently to testify before the City of Los Angeles Mayor's Office of Gang Reduction & Youth Development on the role that TM has played in overcoming the traumas of her life. Here is what she said:

I grew up in a neighbourhood that was known for gang violence. I was influenced by what I thought was cool and started fighting, drinking, using meth and hanging out with a gang. I was thirteen when I was first incarcerated in juvenile hall. Two years later, I was incarcerated again, and then again. I kept getting out, going back home and making the same wrong decisions.

But the fourth time I went home, after I had been locked up for six months, I decided to make a change. I enrolled in New Village Girls Academy. The principal and teachers wanted to know about me – about my past and my journey. It was probably the first time someone actually cared about me.

New Village is also where I learned Transcendental Meditation. Looking back, I see how it changed my life and how it has been essential to my recovery. I am able to take fifteen minutes to focus on myself and not worry about the problems at home, the homework that's due in two days, or that I have to see my parole officer tomorrow. Those fifteen minutes make the rest of my day much better. I feel calmer and less worried. I focus better. I am happier. Life still has not been particularly easy for me. The problems still occur; the stressors are still there. But now I have a technique that helps me to refocus and not lose sight of the big changes I want to make in myself and in my world.

———————— · ————————

PILLAR *three*

CHANGE BEGINS WITHIN

What do you hope to get from learning to meditate?

I often ask that question before I give an introductory talk about the technique.

I hear responses like:

'I love my work, but it is incredibly stressful, and I don't want to burn out.'

'I eat too much, probably because of stress, and I can't stop myself.'

'I have become an anxious, fearful person, and I don't recognize or like myself.'

'I want to relate to people better.'

'My life is going well and I have no particular complaints but I am always interested in learning more, growing more, seeing if there is more to life.'

Maybe one or more of those answers resonate with you.

I remember meeting with Ellen DeGeneres in the living room of her home in Los Angeles. I was there to teach her TM, and I asked her the same question I just asked you: What do you hope to get from learning to meditate? Why now?

'Bob,' she said, and then paused for a moment to think, 'I want to maintain a permanent connection with the intelligence that runs the universe ...'

'Whoa,' I thought to myself.

She waited for one comic beat.

'... and I can't sleep at night.'

I chuckled along with her, but I often think about the truth in both things she said. Ellen encapsulated what so many of us want in our lives. Maybe you don't ask outright for 'the intelligence that runs the universe.' But you want to grow. You want to learn more, do more, and achieve more. It's only natural. You don't want to feel stagnant or stale in your work and relationships. And perhaps most importantly, you don't want to feel stifled within yourself. But the reality is that we are pulled so often in so many directions, taking care of our kids, our partner, our work, it is easy to feel stuck – that we are, at best, spinning our wheels. We are working hard just to keep our head above water, to maintain the status quo. But we are not growing.

What holds us back? Any number of things: Exhaustion. Foggy brain. A shortage of good ideas. Or maybe we don't know what to do, where to start. You can fill in the blanks there for yourself. The point is that meditating gives direct access to your own innermost, unbounded self. In so doing, it gives your body the deep rest it needs to eliminate the buildup of stress and tension that drains energy and undermines health. It makes available the clarity of thinking, the free flow of creative ideas, and the conviction of purpose to create changes in your life and in your world.

I have been teaching people to meditate for a very long time, but I always appreciate seeing the unique way it affects different people. Case in point: when I had the opportunity to teach actor Michael J. Fox. It started when I got a call during halftime while I was attending a New York Knicks game at Madison Square Garden.

It was Tracy Pollan, Michael's wife. She wanted to set up a time for Michael to learn to meditate. As we were hammering out dates, I discussed some of the benefits that the meditation could bring to Michael, who I knew had been battling Parkinson's disease since the early nineties. At the end of the conversation, I asked Tracy offhandedly, 'Is Michael looking forward to learning?'

'Oh, God, he doesn't know,' she said with a laugh. 'I haven't told him yet – it's a surprise!'

Michael must have liked the surprise because he came to our office several weeks later to learn. Before we began, he told me he had not taken any of his medications that day that help to control his tremors. He wanted to see objectively the degree to which meditating calmed him down. Michael on tremor-reducing meds is how you see him on television and in public spaces. Michael off meds is how almost no one sees him, save for his family and closest friends. In fact, after decades with PD, as many people with Parkinson's call it, Michael's tremors had become more pronounced.

I sat across from Michael in my office, both of us in comfortable chairs. I gave him his mantra and explained how to use it properly. He closed his eyes and began to meditate. Within seconds – literally seconds – all his tremors ceased. I am not talking gradually subsided, but just stopped. Stunned by what I saw, I closed my eyes and meditated with him. A few minutes later, when we both were done meditating, I looked over at him, and he was staring at his hands, which lay motionless on his lap. He sat like that for several more minutes, just looking at his hands.

'This moment,' he said, 'is the calmest I have felt in years. Decades.'

I wondered if he would have the same experience the next time he meditated at home. We met the following day, and sure enough, he said the same thing happened. A week later, he told me it was still happening when he meditated at home. Whenever he did TM, the tremors ceased. He said he had begun sleeping more soundly through the night, whereas before he would wake up every one or two hours.

A month later, in another visit, Michael recalled how uncharacteristically relaxed he felt immediately prior to delivering an hour-long talk on Parkinson's before a large audience in Toronto. In the past, he confided, he would have sat backstage, fretting anxiously over every word he planned to say. This time he meditated for twenty minutes in the greenroom, walked out onstage, and gave one of the best talks of his life.

Although Michael's tremors do inevitably return after he finishes his twenty-minute meditation, for him the big thing has been the significant reduction in anxiety levels and the dramatic overall improvement in his quality of life.

Since teaching Michael, I have spoken to many other TM teachers who have taught people with PD to meditate, and they report similar experiences. Why is that happening? It will be interesting to find out. PD is thought to be caused because the brain slowly stops producing the neurotransmitter, or brain chemical, called dopamine. With less and less dopamine, a person has progressively less ability to regulate his or her movements, body and emotions. Perhaps the meditation somehow affects dopamine production, calming this chronic, debilitating neurological disorder. It is the subject of a study the David Lynch Foundation is determined to support.

You can also come at TM as a complete sceptic – like Dr Richard Schneider, a retired rear admiral and president of Norwich University – but still be open to change. I liked President Schneider the moment he greeted me with a firm handshake in his office at Norwich in 2010. Fit, good-natured and affable, he is the longest-serving president of Norwich, the oldest private military college in the United States. President Schneider told me he'd heard about our work through Joan Andrews, the daughter of a beloved NU grad and trustee, the late Paul Andrews.

'You've got to see what TM is doing for veterans,' Joan said. 'It's helping them!'

'Okay, back up, what's TM?' asked President Schneider.

'Transcendental Meditation.'

President Schneider admitted he laughed. Sceptical does not begin to describe how he felt, but he's a smart man, and Norwich has a rep for being on the cutting edge. It was one of the first military colleges to admit women and African Americans. And it's not just about history. This small college in Vermont in the US has worked to be ranked second in the study of cybersecurity, the next field of battle.

'I said, "Okay, let me find out about this,"' he recalled. 'I have a very stressful campus because that's what we do here: we stress them now so they get used to being stressed in the military.'

The more President Schneider learned about the tangible benefits of the meditation, the more interested he was. So he invited me and my colleague Colonel Brian Rees, a medical doctor who served five tours in Iraq and Afghanistan, to meet with him and his whole administrative team, and talk about starting a pilot programme teaching TM.

'I support the idea of the programme,' he told me at the time. 'But I have to learn myself before I suggest it to any student. I have to lead from the front.'

He knew he could be taking a big risk in bringing meditation to a military college, 'professionally and reputationally,' he told me. 'I needed to learn so I could look people in the eye and say, "I'm doing this. It works for me."'

On a cool, sunny afternoon in a private study room off the university's main library hall, I taught him how to meditate. Within days of learning, President Schneider found that his life was less stressful even though none of the usual external stressors had disappeared. 'I was more centered, and I was more relaxed,' he said. 'I stopped sweating the small stuff, and I think it's the small stuff that drives you crazy.' He enjoys meditating on planes, he added, because he has the experience of all the noise just fading away – 'even when some kid behind me is kicking the chair. I'm aware of it, but I am perfectly relaxed.'

President Schneider saw the potential value for the 'rooks': the incoming cadets. 'Cadets have been arriving at Norwich with more and more stress,' he said. 'Any of our counselling staff would tell you the same thing. And once you hear these kids' stories, it's no wonder they can't focus on their calculus. They have so much other baggage in the way.'

Just out of high school, many of these leaders-in-training are worried about their single parents, and what is happening to their younger brothers and sisters in their neighbourhoods. 'It's usually not about themselves,' President Schneider explained. 'They're worried about others.'

He announced the TM pilot programme in a letter to the inbound class and the youngsters' parents. 'We got overrun with parents who wanted their kids to try it,' he said. 'We did a control group of a platoon of about thirty kids who got the training, and thirty of those who didn't.

'Honestly, within three weeks, the kids who didn't get the training were complaining like they were disadvantaged,' said President Schneider. 'Because the meditating kids weren't getting yelled at, they were staying awake in class, they were performing better. So they wanted it. And I told them, "You'll get it but you're going to have to wait."'

In every measurable functional area, the TM team was outperforming the control team. Issues such as depression, anxiety, stress, bad moods – all went down significantly. Constructive thinking, emotional coping and resilience all went up.

'I have an ethical responsibility to provide anything I can give these young people to be more successful and more victorious and take better care of their troops,' he told me. President Schneider feels an added responsibility knowing that he is training future officers who will be charged not just with managing their own stress in adversity but also that of the people they lead. 'If the leader is stressed, everybody in the team knows it,' he said. 'You want the team to be confident.'

*   *   *

Resilience in the midst of dire situations: that is certainly what's needed during a typical night in the emergency room at Chicago's Mount Sinai Hospital. One of four top-level trauma centres in Chicago, Sinai is also at the centre of West Side gang turf.

And right there in the middle of it is Dr John Vazquez, chief medical officer of Sinai Group and chair of anaesthesiology. 'Summer is busier,' he told me. 'We have a higher amount of trauma during the warmer months.'

Sinai is a level-1 trauma centre, which is the highest severity, and a level-3 neonatal intensive care unit, which is also the highest severity. 'We see the sickest of the sick, and we can see very severe trauma,' said Dr Vazquez. 'The violence is certainly devastating for the families. But it's also traumatic for the first responders, the people in the ambulance, and the people who receive that person in the emergency and operating rooms.'

To help manage stress, Dr Vazquez began practising TM a couple of years back through a training grant offered to the hospital. I was particularly interested in Dr Vazquez's experience because he not only handles the pressures of an operating room but also understands the boardroom. 'I've got a dual role here. I am an anaesthesiologist by training, so that's clinical,' he explained. 'I'm also chief medical officer of the medical group, which has over three hundred medical group physicians. That part of my job can be the business part. In addition to running a department, I oversee the business part of the medical group. I have a lot of demands on my time.'

Dr Vazquez can see the effects of trauma from a personal standpoint and has a managerial sense of how it is affecting the staff. The week before we spoke, Dr Vazquez spoke of a trauma case he took care of personally. 'It is incredibly sad to see people lose their life at such an early age and the loss of such great potential.

'It can cause burnout,' he said, adding, 'I've seen physicians decide to leave the acute care hospital setting and choose to practise in a more outpatient basis to reduce the stress level.'

Dr Vazquez loves his work, loves serving his community. He says that meditating helps keep some of the stress of his job at bay. 'But I think some of the trauma stays with you,' he admitted. 'There's no way you can experience what we see and have it not impact you. But meditating is a powerful tool that helps me manage the stress and prevent it from taking a toll.'

I can't highlight these stories of personal transformation and healing without telling you about Joey Lowenstein. I had never taught a child who is on the autism spectrum until a few years ago. But I had heard from fellow TM teachers that kids and adults with autism benefit from meditating.

Then Joey came into my life. His mum, Roberta Lowenstein, reached out to me after she had been meditating for two years. She explained the severity of the condition of her son, then fifteen. He was non-verbal but communicated with a letter board. His IQ is off the charts genius level, but he can't sit still. Worse, he has terrible anxiety.

That's key to understanding his story. He has a disability, but the separate issue is his anxiety.

'Will you teach him?' his mum asked.

'Of course,' I said.

When we met to begin instruction, right away I saw that Joey had serious issues with attention. In fact, for the first week or so after he learned to meditate, he could keep his eyes closed only for a minute or two before he would jump up out of his chair. But Joey has a genuineness about him that people love – myself included. We stuck it out, Roberta either brought Joey by my office for follow-up visits or else I met with Joey at their apartment so that he was in a familiar environment.

He began to feel like family to me, and I wanted to see him succeed.

And we got there. Within a month or so, Joey was

meditating for fifteen minutes twice a day and really enjoying the benefits. His mum said he was less anxious and displaying more self-confidence. She recalled the time Joey was stuck in a lift in a New York City high-rise for almost an hour with only his caregiver and a bottle of water.

'TM is what got Joey through that frightening experience,' Roberta told me. 'He started out calm and stayed that way.'

Yes, Joey has challenges, and he is keenly aware of them. But he is a normal teenage boy: he wants a girl-friend; he wants friends. And feeling socially awkward had left him with the impression that he didn't measure up.

That sounds like a lot of us, right? I remember asking him during one visit how his meditation was going. He wrote back on his letter board that he was really loving his practice. So I asked why.

'Because it's so easy,' he wrote back. 'I can do it.'

'Of course you can,' I replied. 'But what makes you love it?'

'It's the only time during the day,' he wrote, 'that I don't feel bad about myself.'

It was tough to see those words spelled out so clearly. Since that conversation, Roberta and Joey moved to Georgia, where he is enjoying a more supportive environment for his continued growth. Roberta said that Joey is starting to talk more and more and is growing in self-assurance. She credits his regular TM practice as a contributing factor – and Joey agrees. He also says that meditating keeps his mum in better spirits.

'TM calms the mind and the mum,' he wrote to me one afternoon on his letter board after the three of us had meditated together.

Obviously, TM brought tangible benefits to Joey's life. So can TM help teens who are not on the spectrum develop resilience and the ability to function well in stressful circumstances? Can it help the highly stressed-out high achiever and the unmotivated underachiever?

There is no doubt that it can, says Dr William Stixrud, one of the leading clinical neuropsychologists in the US. Dr Stixrud is also a member of the adjunct faculty of the Children's National Medical Center, in Washington, DC, and an assistant professor of psychiatry at the George Washington University School of Medicine and Health Sciences. Additionally, he is the coauthor of the upcoming *The Self-Driven Child: The Science and Sense of Giving Kids More Control Over Their Lives*. I spoke with Dr Stixrud because he is an expert in how parents and other adults can help young people 'sculpt' brains that work effectively – what he calls 'stretching kids without breaking them.'

Although teens don't often ask their parents to find them a TM teacher – usually because they've never heard of the technique before – when they do meditate regularly, it benefits kids in the same ways that it does adults. Like adults, young people have a centre – a core that is peaceful and happy – which they learn to access through TM, says Dr Stixrud. 'And the more they do it, the more they find that they are calmer and less reactive to stress. And when they do get stressed, it goes away faster – often twice as fast as it does in kids who don't meditate. Kids who meditate generally sleep better, are more able to keep things in perspective, and more generally find it easier to get through life with less wear and tear.'

This is true for kids handling the stress of growing up in extreme poverty, and it is also true for children from wealthy families who feel tremendous pressure at elite schools. Dr Stixrud recently presented at a conference at which several professionals discussed data showing that TM is a powerful tool for preventing violence in disadvantaged youth. At one point in the conference, a woman who directs a high school programme for high-performing students, many of whom are very stressed, told the audience that she had introduced TM into her school because 'I couldn't stand to send one more depressed or self-harming kid to the hospital.'

Research has also shown that TM can give virtually any teen the power to think twice – or even once – before acting. It helps impulsive kids be more thoughtful, and it helps emotionally reactive kids to tone down their responses. As Dr Stixrud says, 'TM allows their brain's prefrontal cortex to better modulate their amygdala, which gives them a greater sense of control.'

Dr Stixrud likes to tell the story of a particularly hyperactive and impulsive young teenager he met during a TM study. The boy was, along with his fellow students at a school for kids with learning disabilities, three months into his practice of meditation, and Dr Stixrud was doing a routine check-in to record results.

'Are you feeling any effects from meditation in your day-to-day life?' he asked. The teenager paused for a minute, clearly giving the question some thought. 'It used to be if I'd be walking through the halls and someone bumped into me, I'd just turn around and hit him.'

Dr Stixrud nodded, ever the professional.

'But now that I've been meditating, if somebody bumps me while I'm walking in the halls, I stop and think, "Should I hit him or not?"' Dr Stixrud told me that after he stopped laughing, he had the following thought: 'Getting impulsive kids to be less impulsive is really hard; this may be the best thing anyone's ever told me about Transcendental Meditation!'

That kid in the hall is like a lot of us, though for you and me, the question is less likely to be 'Should I hit him or not?' but 'Should I overreact and reply to this email and show everyone this person's a fool?' Meditating gives you the time and the space to react and make wise decisions, not just in the moment but also in figuring out big-picture concerns, such as what do you really want from life?

I find that many people are able to see the value of meditation in their own lives when they see what it does for veterans. 'If the technique can work for these men and women who live with the most toxic levels of stress and anxiety,' the thinking goes, 'then maybe it could work for me.'

So, meet Melanie Pote. She was eighteen months into her service in the US Army when everything went wrong. Around seven in the morning on 20 March, 2002, she was finishing her night watch of ammunition at Fort Drum in upstate New York. It was training week, and Melanie and other members of the 110th Military Intelligence Battalion were getting ready for a day of rifle practice on a nearby range. But first they had to line up for breakfast at the mess tent.

'Because I guarded the ammo at night, I was usually first in line, right at seven o'clock,' Melanie told me. 'But for some reason, I kept stalling. The guy who relieved me said, "Come on, it's been fifteen minutes. Get going." So I did.'

At 7:20, Melanie was fifth in line when two artillery shells fell far short of their drill target and sent shrapnel ripping through the mess tent. The cannon shells, each with the power to rip apart a tank, were fired after members of another battalion 'acted in a negligent manner,' according to Fort Drum's then acting commander.

'We saw the shells coming,' Melanie recalled. 'And then there was the explosion. The first person in line was killed instantly. That's where I usually was. And another sergeant whom I knew very well was killed. He didn't die right away. He died later. But I watched him struggle as we tried to take care of him.'

Melanie was thrown through the air. 'I didn't even realize I was hurt,' she said. 'I was trying to help everyone else. Then I saw I had two pieces of shrapnel in my left leg.'

Her wounds healed, but the trauma remained. 'You just don't plan for that on your own base,' she said. 'You plan for it over there, in Iraq.' Melanie went home, and things only got worse. 'From my experience with military PTSD, there's a lot of triggers. There are so many noises that happen – a car backfiring or fireworks – that will bring up a previous event.'

Worse, even the anticipation of being triggered caused Melanie to live in a clenched state of panic. 'I had tightness in my chest and pain there all the time,' she said. After a decade of feeling untethered, Melanie, now a tattoo artist working out of Lawrenceville, Georgia, sought the expertise of a therapist who helped her work through her survivor's guilt. Still, she lived with that inescapable fear. 'For a long, long time,' she said, 'I was very lost.'

Yet here she was now, a shy but funny young woman, talking to me. What started the change? 'You're gonna laugh, but I heard about meditation from an interview with the actor Matt Bomer,' she told me. 'He said something like, "Everyone needs a reset button so you can start your day without anxiety."'

Curious, Melanie looked into TM in 2016 and decided to learn. 'Within two weeks of practice, I was driving my car down the road, and I realized, "Wait, I don't have any tightness in my chest. I don't have any chest pain. I don't have that constant feeling of dread that I am going to die."' She pulled over and called her meditation teacher. 'I was laughing because it seemed so crazy. I'd lived with this anxiety for so long, and meditation was the missing piece to heal it.'

There are moments, of course, where Melanie's trauma returns, but the effects are not as severe, and it dissipates more quickly, she said. 'I can't stand fireworks, but that constant dread isn't there. It's been replaced with more of a calm.'

You can put Melanie's story in further context with this sobering fact: according to a recent study from the US Department of Veterans Affairs, twenty-one American military veterans commit suicide *a day*. That means that while veterans make up only 9 per cent of the population, they account for double – 18 per cent – the number of US suicides. The study includes more than fifty million veterans' records from 1979 to 2014 from every state. Most striking, roughly 65 per cent of all veteran suicides in 2014 were for individuals fifty years or older, many of whom spent little or no time fighting in the most recent wars.[1] A half million US troops deployed since 2001 have PTSD in return for their service. The Rand Center for Military Health Policy Research estimated that costs related to PTSD and depression could range from $4 billion to $6.2 billion over two years.[2]

In the UK over 400 active duty military personnel committed suicide between 1995 and 2014, which is more than died in combat over all those years. (Unlike the US government, the British government does not record suicide rates among veterans.) And suicide statistics from the Australian Institute of Health and Welfare from 2001 to 2014 show twice as many defence force personnel took their own lives compared to the national rate.

The first study of TM as a treatment for post-traumatic stress involved combat veterans of the Vietnam War. The trial showed a 52 per cent reduction in anxiety symptoms, a 46 per cent drop in depression, and a 40 per cent reduction in symptoms of post-traumatic stress after three months' practice of the technique. Veterans who couldn't sleep finally found relief, and many who'd turned to alcohol abuse were able to ease off their drinking.[3]

More recently, a study of vets from the wars in Iraq and Afghanistan showed a 48 per cent reduction in symptoms of post-traumatic stress, and an 87 per cent improvement in depression. The results were evident after just two months of practising TM.[4]

In 2010 the David Lynch Foundation began offering TM to veterans, active-duty military per-sonnel, and cadets – and their families – through our Operation Warrior Wellness initiative. That's how Paul Downs learned to meditate. In his eleven years serving as an infantryman in the US Marine Corps,

Paul was deployed in hotspots and combat zones throughout the world. In the Middle East alone, he served in Iraq, Oman, Qatar and Kuwait. When Paul left the marines, one of the things he looked forward to most was being close to his young children. But what he didn't realize was just how much his identity as a marine meant to him. When Paul left the Corps, he said, he lost pretty much everything: his tribe, his sense of self, and all that he knew to be true. Because of that, he lost his sense of forward momentum, purpose and connection.

Paul suffered from PTSD. To outside observers, he told me, he might have seemed like 'just another angry, disgruntled veteran.' He sought help from the Veterans Administration, looking for guidance, direction and connection. He says nothing helped. He quit trying.

'I was drowning in fear and sadness,' he reflected. 'A few months after putting away the uniform, I developed a pretty detailed plan for suicide. But while sitting in my truck, ready to proceed, a thought hit me: to die by my own hand is not my birthright. It is not the way of the warrior. Warriors have a deep appreciation for life and are not victims of circumstance.'

Desperate, Paul reached out to the Boulder Crest Retreat in Virginia, a highly respected residential centre for veterans, active-duty military, and first responders seeking to heal the hidden wounds of trauma. There he learned Transcendental Meditation.

'What I learned at Boulder Crest was excellent, but much of it didn't apply to everyday life outside of the retreat centre, like equine therapy or archery,' he told me. 'TM is different. You can take it anywhere and do it anytime: at home, on an airplane, sitting in traffic, anywhere. Veterans need this meditation. We need to learn how to regulate so we can be calm, cool and collected at home, just like we were trained to be on the battlefield. TM has worked for me, and it has worked for thousands of my brothers and sisters. It's given me the opportunity not just to survive on earth but to thrive here – and to live a life that is truly full of purpose, meaning, connection and service.'

Five years ago, the US Department of Defense funded a $2.4 million clinical trial to evaluate the effects of the Transcendental Meditation programme on the severity of trauma symptoms as well as depression when compared with cognitive behavioural therapy (working to change patterns of behaviour to alleviate symptoms) with prolonged exposure (allowing the person to be exposed to the feared object without danger), and health education. The randomized, controlled study, conducted at the VA San Diego Healthcare System, enrolled 203 veterans with documented post-traumatic stress.

Results presented to the Military Health System Research Symposium in August 2017 showed that both the TM group and the group offered prolonged-exposure therapy, which has been considered the gold standard for PTSD treatment, significantly decreased trauma symptom severity and depression compared with health education after three months. What's more, the benefits were generally higher in the TM group compared with those who underwent prolonged exposure.

Dr Sandy Nidich, co-principal investigator of the study, told me, 'Transcendental Meditation is a nontrauma-focused treatment and may actually be preferable to other treatments for PTSD, such as exposure therapy, that involve repeated, deliberate contact with anxiety-provoking stimuli.'

MY OWN STORY

I can't really ask you to think about what you might get from learning to meditate without telling you what TM has done for me.

I grew up in the San Francisco Bay Area in the 1950s and 1960s, inheriting a passion for education from my schoolteacher mother and a deep respect for science and a healthy dose of scepticism from my radiologist father. Dad put himself through medical school in Detroit delivering newspapers during the Depression and then went off to serve during the Second World War as a medic on the front lines of Europe. He came back with a smashed right hip and chronic pain in his hip, knee and back for the rest of his life. The US surgeon general operated on Dad's hip three times and blew each one of the surgeries.

During one stint, he was in a body cast for nine months at Walter Reed Hospital in Washington, DC. Nine months in severe pain in a body cast with no air conditioning in the stifling heat of Washington. I can't imagine.

I knew this only from my mother, because my father never, ever talked about anything from the war. As a kid, I found a box of his medals and was excited to ask about them. He shifted uncomfortably in his chair, looked away, and changed the subject like I'd shown him an old box of musty smelling rocks. In fact, none of my friends' dads – almost all of them veterans – ever discussed what they'd seen.

Dad was hired as assistant chief of radiology at the Veterans Administration Hospital at Fort Miley in San Francisco, which sat on a spectacular vista right at the intersection of the Pacific Ocean and the San Francisco Bay. So my parents, my older sister, Ellen, and I moved across the country – first to San Francisco for a few months and then across the Golden Gate Bridge to Greenbrae in Marin County. Within a few years, my brothers, Bill and Tom, were born. In many regards, it felt like we were a military family. Because my dad was a captain when he was injured, we could shop at the post exchange supermarket at Hamilton Air Force Base, a thirty-minute drive in traffic north in Novato. It was fairly inconvenient to get there, but it saved a lot of money.

As reserved as my dad could be, my mum was the most expansive and loving woman. She had this thing about keeping a constant open house. She knew people at the United Nations office in San Francisco who would call her if a foreign diplomat needed a place to stay. My siblings and I would wake up in the morning to find that a finance minister from Ghana would be living with us for three months. She was the emergency call for any foreign exchange student in need of a last-minute placement.

Because of Dad's constant pain from his war injuries, my parents put a swimming pool in the backyard for his therapy. If you knew my mum, you could guess what happened. She was a special education volunteer at Marindale School for kids with physical and intellectual disadvantages. She invited her students over for frequent pool-day field trips. When she saw how happy that made them, she reached out to an inner-city school in Marin City, organizing visits for them. Sometimes I would come home from school, and there would be a busload of forty African American kids in the garden swimming and having fun.

Dad hoped I'd be a doctor, but it wasn't for me. When I was ten, he tried to get me interested in medicine by bringing me along to Fort Miley. Saturday mornings, he'd find me playing basketball in the back garden. 'Okay, Bobby,' he'd say, 'we're going to go to the hospital, and I'm going to read one X-ray. Then we'll go to Candlestick Park.'

Candlestick was where my beloved San Francisco Giants played. The idea of going to a Giants game was it for me. So I would go to Fort Miley and sit in the hospital waiting room. Invariably, one X-ray would become two, and then ten, and then too many for me to count, because there were always emergencies. I used to sit there for hours. And I watched these war-torn, sad-faced vets rolling up and down the sterile corridors in wheelchairs and bandages. Broken men. Seeing their physical and emotional pain left a deep impression on my heart. Maybe that's why I am drawn so much to work with veterans today.

My dad also started volunteering once a week to read X-rays at San Quentin State Prison, a few miles from our home. Believe it or not, there was a restaurant on the prison grounds staffed by inmates, who were called 'trustees.' So once or twice a month, my parents would take my sister and brothers and me to dinner there because, surprise, it was less expensive to feed a family of six at a prison restaurant. Now, if you were incarcerated at San Quentin, you were there for something brutal and violent – often murder. But the trustee staff became human to me, and I particularly remember a waiter named Tommy, this big guy who was missing his middle two fingers on his left hand. Tommy always remembered my order: chicken-fried steak.

Of course, once my friends found out about my prison visits, they all wanted to go. The big thing was to go to my house after school on a Friday, go out to dinner at San Quentin with my family, and then return home to watch *The Twilight Zone* on TV and spend the night. After lights out, my friends would dream up the crazy scenarios that must have got the guys into prison. I'd play along, but I really began to wonder what horrible things they had been through in their lives that landed them behind bars.

Probably because of my upbringing, at an early age I had a fascination with politics and was drawn to public service as a career. Like most of the kids I grew up with, I loved President John F. Kennedy. I remember in the spring of 1963 joining my Boy Scout troop to take up President Kennedy's fitness challenge to hike fifty miles. Even then I knew I was a very fortunate kid growing up amidst the coastal mountains of the northern Bay Area. As often as I could, I'd hike and camp outdoors on Mount Tamalpais. By October 1963, I had turned thirteen, become an Eagle Scout, and fallen in love with Denise Biancalana, my first girlfriend.

And then President Kennedy was assassinated. Looking back, I'm sure it traumatized much of the country on a deep level, most especially the kids. It certainly shocked to the core this thirteen-year-old boy who didn't really know what death was. And I remember feeling so awful and wondering how it was possible that the sun could come up tomorrow. How can things just continue?

It did, though it was not the same. In Autumn 1967, my senior year in high school, I, along with so many other kids at that time, woke up to a world in turmoil. Like so many people, I had become enamoured by President Kennedy's brother Bobby, when he became a senator from New York. His vision became my vision: to create a more equitable and just world. It wasn't that I identified closely as a Democrat or Republican. I didn't. I just wanted things to be better. I was accepted into the University of California at Berkeley in October 1968, and my plan was to eventually attend UC Berkeley's law school, become a lawyer, and then become a US senator, like Bobby Kennedy. I thought the way to improve people's lives would be through politics and changing public policy.

During the summer before my university classes started, I used to tutor a twelve-year-old African American kid, Kenny. He was from a poor family that lived in public housing in Marin City. I would help Kenny, focusing mostly on the reading skills he hadn't been getting at school. It was just Kenny and his mum, and I became close with them both. On one visit, I borrowed my dad's Nikon camera and took their portrait. I developed the black-and-white photos myself and gave his mum this big nine-by-thirteen-inch horizontal shot. She loved it. But as I developed the picture and looked at this beautiful, smiling mother and son, I stood there wondering what would happen to Kenny. This wasn't new. I would see Kenny once a week and think about him the rest of the time. He wasn't learning much at school, and the world seemed hell-bent on telling him not to bother.

I was able to see Senator Kennedy speak in person at the San Francisco Civic Auditorium on 1 June 1968. I remember the crooner Bobby Darin sang 'Mack the Knife' at the rally. And then Senator Kennedy spoke, and I felt I was part of something that could make a difference. It felt good.

Then, four days later, Bobby Kennedy was assassinated at the Ambassador Hotel in Los Angeles. Coming just two months after the slaying of Dr Martin Luther King, Jr., the feelings of loss for this idealistic seventeen-year-old were almost too much to bear.

That first year at Berkeley was very tough. The university was in a state of constant upheaval, with war protests devolving into riots. There were helicopters spewing tear gas overhead and tactical police and National Guard tanks parked outside my dorm. I remember walking home from a physics class on College Avenue and hearing a thunder of feet behind me. I turned around, and there were thirty Oakland tactical police waving billy clubs, chasing *me*. I had done nothing wrong. Luckily, I ran much faster than they did.

I was eighteen, and the first year of college is supposed to be tumultuous anyway. But with all the unrest on campus, mine was tumult on steroids. For the first time in my privileged young life, I had an inkling of what it was like to feel unsettled, disconnected and unsafe. Even small things started to worry me, and outsized reactions to small events just built on each other.

Everyone at school seemed to fall into a group: left, right, hippie, athlete, or religious fanatic. I was none of them. I didn't take drugs, and I couldn't relate to the political polarization on either side. I was just a guy who thought he was going to transition smoothly from a suburban high school to university life and then help make a difference in the world.

The brutally divisive 1968 presidential race between Richard Nixon and Vice President Hubert Humphrey left me disillusioned with pursuing politics as a career path. Inspired by my mother's love of teaching and memories of working with Kenny and his mum, I decided that I would pursue a doctorate in education instead. My plan was to specialize in developing educational curricula to help underserved children not just learn the basics, such as algebra, but also to acquire social and emotional tools to survive and, hopefully, rise above their challenging (to say the least) circumstances. I fervently agreed with the Irish poet William Butler Yeats, who wrote, 'Education is not about filling the pail, it is about lighting a fire.'

While I worked toward that goal, I had a stint to earn some extra cash at a Swensen's Ice Cream parlour on Durant Avenue. It was just north of Telegraph Avenue, where street demonstrations against the Vietnam War were almost a daily occurrence. And it was at Swensen's that I met a coworker named Peter Stevens.

Peter was twenty-six, with a master's degree from Tufts University near Boston, and he was studying landscape design on his own. He worked part-time at Swensen's for the spending money, and people of all sorts liked him because at Berkeley he was about the only person who seemed down-to-earth and normal – which in Berkeley in 1968 was high praise.

I'd worked with Peter about six months when, one evening around ten o'clock, I took a break from studying and went into Swensen's to get some ice cream. I knew Peter was working the late shift, but he was nowhere in sight.

'Where's Peter?' I asked another worker.

'Oh, he's in the back meditating,' she said.

'What?'

Just the word *meditating* struck me like an electric shock. It had such a bizarre connotation and really wasn't even in my vocabulary. But when he walked out to the front of the store, there he was, just Peter, but a little brighter than usual, smiling a little more, with a little more serenity on his kind face. I took notice.

I asked what he was doing, and he told me he practised Transcendental Meditation. Of course, I had heard about it because the press had made such a big deal of the Beatles going off to India to study TM with Maharishi in early 1968.

Sitting in one place with my eyes closed meditating had never been very appealing to me. I saw myself as a doer; a get-it-done kind of a guy. I wanted to change the world, and that required *action*. I also thought maybe it was a philosophy or religion, and I just wasn't into that.

On the other hand, I was pretty stressed out, and I did respect Peter a lot. I found myself curious. I asked him to tell me more. He pointed me in the direction of the TM centre on Channing Way, one block south of College Avenue, and a few blocks east of campus. I knew the building. The sign on the outside of it read, in all caps, STUDENTS INTERNATIONAL MEDITATION SOCIETY. I had walked past it many times on my way from my Putnam Hall dorm, heading to my sister, Ellen's apartment on Hillside Court in the Berkeley Hills.

I decided to trust Peter, take a leap and attend what was billed as an introductory lecture. The three-story white-stucco building had a spacious lecture hall with about thirty chairs lined up theatre-style in rows. I felt comfortable. It was a normal place. There were no pillows to sit on and no holding hands in a group.

A woman in her late twenties gave the talk, and she ran through the basics of the practice and its benefits. At the end, she asked if there were questions. I raised my hand, and asked, 'This all sounds good, but how much do I have to believe for it to work?'

The woman nodded amiably. Then she held up a piece of chalk in her right hand. She waited a moment and then dropped the chalk into her outstretched left hand below.

'You don't have to believe in gravity for this chalk to fall,' she said. 'Like that, you don't have to believe in anything to practise TM.' In fact, she said, I could be 100 per cent sceptical, and the technique would work just fine.

That clicked with me. I liked that I could be a sceptic and didn't have to 'believe' in Transcendental Meditation for it to work. The only firm conviction I had about it, in fact, was that I was going to be the one person who would be unable to meditate. She assured me that everyone has this nagging suspicion, and yes, anyone can learn.

Two days later, on the sunny Saturday morning of 28 June 1969, I returned to the TM centre to start the course.

Sylvia Schmidt was my teacher. She was in her early thirties, a soft-spoken academic. I walked with her into the small instruction room on the second floor of the centre.

'Okay, I'm here,' I thought to myself as I settled into a comfortable chair to her left.

As Sylvia led me through the beginning steps of instruction, I felt my mind and body sinking into a state of deep relaxation. Now, remember, I was a tightly wound, sceptical eighteen-year-old kid. And yet within seconds of my first experience meditating, I felt this wave of physiological peace come over me. The tension in my neck, shoulders and stomach muscles were the first to go – and my racing mind settled down. Yet I was fully aware, fully awake. It was both unique and as familiar and natural as could be. Once the meditation was over, I remember thinking to myself, 'This is *something*. It's not just my imagination or visualizing, this is really *something*.'

One of my next thoughts was 'I would like to teach this to kids.'

I learned quickly that TM was judgement free. There were no hidden strings. No organization to join, no ongoing dues to pay, no pressure to buy anything. Sylvia told me to meditate again later that afternoon. I was supposed to study at Ellen's place. I didn't want my sister to know just yet that I'd begun meditating, so I told her I was going out in her garden to read. I had this bright idea to try the meditation on this little deck tucked away on the hillside. There was no chair, so I sat on the wooden planks. And I meditated. *And* I was eaten alive by mosquitoes. I mean eaten alive. I realized then and there you don't have to sit outside to find nature. From then on, when people say, 'Oh, let's meditate outside,' I think, 'Hmm, a room with a chair is nice, too.'

I told my family and they began to notice changes. Ellen started six months after I did. When two Roths were the better for it, a month later my parents and my brothers, Bill and Tom, started.

Now I had the satisfaction of seeing, in these people I'd known and loved all my life, just how TM made them feel better, happier, more themselves. My parents continued to meditate until their passing, and my sister and brothers are still at it decades later. In fact, Ellen, who raised two boys and who now spends a lot of time with her grandchildren, and Tom, who runs a market research firm and volunteers to bring TM to people living with HIV, also studied to become TM teachers back in the early 1970s and both continue to teach today. Bill, a builder of green homes and small office buildings, has been a regular meditator since 1970.

Seeing what TM could do for the people I loved, I realized I wanted to be able to teach others. In 1972 I heard there was a teacher-training course with Maharishi in Mallorca, Spain. Maharishi instructed me and thousands of others about how to teach people to meditate. I loved hearing the discussions, which could evolve into hours and hours, about the deep connections between an ancient science of consciousness and the modern sciences of quantum physics, neuroscience, biochemistry and psychology. The conversations felt timeless, and were both abstract and practical. After I was certified as a teacher, I headed back to the Bay Area, where I taught TM to the public as well as in local schools, businesses and government agencies.

But one of my most searing memories of that time was teaching guards and inmates at San Quentin Prison. I was able to get back there because of a Hells Angel who was doing time in Folsom State Prison. His name was Pat Corum, and he was a self-confessed murderer. George Ellis, a close friend of mine and a TM instructor, had launched the TM-in-prison programme in the mid-1970s. He went to Folsom to teach Pat, and it helped him so much that this Hells Angel went from being the drug connection in prison to the meditation connection. Pat asked George to teach more inmates, and with the results there, the case was made to bring it into San Quentin. Some amazing research was published showing a 50 per cent reduction in recidivism rates. And when you consider that as much as 80 per cent of all crime is from repeat offenders, I could see even back then the potential impact Transcendental Meditation could have in an overburdened criminal justice system.

Let me take you inside the walls at San Quentin back in the early 1980s: if you had to be there for an eight o'clock evening meeting, you needed to arrive at six because it took about two hours of pat downs and metal detectors and signed waivers. There was a lot of sitting on old, banged-up metal folding chairs in old, paint-peeled rooms. You'd have to go through four massive gates, and at each one, you had to sign something that basically said, 'If you are taken hostage, the prison will not negotiate for your release.'

I remember one night in 1981. It was in a bare, windowless meeting room, and I was there for a refresher course with inmates who had already learned to meditate. There were about thirty men, most too young or too old to be there, sitting in the metal chairs. They were of every race but dressed identically in blue jeans and blue work shirts. The guard for the group was a Baptist minister who was also a meditator.

After the meditation, another guard, who had stood

by watching the whole thing, came up to me. 'That was a first,' he said.

I thought he was being sarcastic about meditation, but there was no smirk on his face.

'Nowhere else in prison have I ever seen those particular guys sit together in the same room and close their eyes,' he continued. 'Not in the dining hall. Nowhere.'

Because if you closed your eyes in San Quentin, he explained, you could end up with a shiv in your back.

'Do you realize,' he asked, 'that you just had the Aryan Brotherhood, Mexican Mafia, and the Black Panthers all in the same room?'

We called that prison programme in San Quentin Freedom Behind Bars.

———— • ————

MEDITATIVE MOMENT
Developing the Intangible for Greatness

Tony Spinosa is director of Health and Fitness at National Defense University, a graduate-level institution in Washington, DC, for members of the US Armed Forces. NDU was established to prepare military and civilian leaders to anticipate and counter emerging security threats with a rigorous study of military strategy, global engagement and tech research.

Before joining NDU, Tony served 20 years in the US Army and retired as a Lieutenant Colonel in 1999. He coached freshman football at West Springfield High School in Northern Virginia, earned a master's degree at George Mason University, and was then hired as the strength coach for the Washington Redskins professional football team under Coach Joe Gibbs. A few years later, he accepted the fitness leadership role at NDU because it would allow him, he said, to expand the definition of fitness to include a mental and spiritual element as well as physical conditioning.

Tony's focus at National Defense University is to provide the tools and techniques to promote life-long health and fitness to his students, most of whom are in their early 40s and 50s, and many of whom will go on to become generals and admirals in the US military. He also mentors NDU faculty and staff.

We work on three aspects of fitness. First is diet and exercise. We work with individuals who have metabolic syndrome, high cholesterol and other health issues. Second, we work in the areas of cognitive performance, enhancing memory and focus. And third, we promote spiritual wellness. That means we deal with the intangibles of who we are, what drives us to succeed, and what moves us to achieve greatness.

I always wanted to bring meditation into the NDU curriculum to promote all three areas of our concern. I did a lot of reading up on the science of meditation. I tried several different types of mindfulness techniques and guided meditations. Personally, I didn't find them easy to do – I couldn't get my brain to rest or my mind to settle down. Then last year my thoracic surgeon, Dr Hassan Tetteh, suggested I try Transcendental Meditation. So I started and I found it to be incredibly easy to learn and practise. It has already done great things for me. I am able to focus a lot better, think more clearly, and I'm less anxious – I don't get stressed out over situations and circumstances that used to bother me.

Before offering TM to my students I was sure there would be some scepticism, some resistance. It was the opposite. I was surprised at how many were already educated, already open. Of the 600 graduate-level students, more than one hundred learned TM within the first several weeks of the new school year – and there is now a sizeable waiting list for others to start as well.

What I appreciate about TM is that it rests and rejuvenates a part of my brain that ordinarily never gets rest. The morning meditation gets me ready for the day and the afternoon meditation clears out the stress of the day from my brain and body. My wife learned, too, and we meditate together whenever we can.

I love teaching people to meditate, all sorts of people, but working with kids has always had a special place in my life. Because, going back to my roots, if you want to create a better world, it has to begin with young people. I found someone of like mind in 2004. He was the great filmmaker, painter, musician, woodworker, sculptor and longtime TM practitioner David Lynch, who you just met a few pages back. We became fast friends, like brothers, first working together on a project to build a large meditation centre in LA. Several months later, I spoke with David and Dr John Hagelin, a Harvard-trained quantum physicist, who heads up the TM organization in the United States, of my long-standing desire to bring TM to young people.

'Let's start a foundation,' I said.

'Good idea,' David and John agreed.

'We should put it in your name, David,' I replied.

'All right,' he said.

'Can I send out a press release to announce the David Lynch Foundation?'

'Sure,' he said, most likely thinking not much would come of it.

The press release was picked up by the major wire services, and within a few days, news stories of the formation of the David Lynch Foundation began appearing in thousands of newspapers all over the world.

It was really as simple as that. No great forethought. No five-year business plan. No money, even. Just a genuine shared desire to do something good for the world. And so much good has come of it – and so much of it due to David's true genius: his extraordinary creativity, conviction, and energy.

David's foundation was born on 21 July 2005, in partnership with Dr Hagelin and the TM organization. For the first few years, we offered the meditation to whatever school or organization wanted it. So if a school for American Indian teens living on an impoverished reservation outside of Lincoln, Nebraska, wanted a programme, we would raise the money and pay for it. Or if there was a prison willing to let us come in, we would go and find a way to fund it. So it was with urban schools in crime-ridden neighbourhoods, women's shelters, veterans' service organizations and HIV clinics in the United States and abroad.

In April 2009 the David Lynch Foundation hosted our first benefit concert at New York's Radio City Music Hall with headliners Paul McCartney and Ringo Starr, along with Donovan, Mike Love of the Beach Boys, Jerry Seinfeld, Howard Stern and many others. Our goal: to raise the funds to teach one million at-risk youth around the world to meditate.

We were sure the announcement would be greeted

with great positivity and fanfare among the New York City philanthropic community. Wrong. The complaints poured into our office: 'Why are Paul and Ringo wasting their time performing for meditation?' The concert came right after the 2008 financial collapse, and the feeling among many in New York was that with philanthropic dollars scarce, why drain them off for something as frivolous as meditation for kids? What about raising money to build more schools, cure malaria, end poverty? All genuine questions that demanded answers. At the time, we were working with a wonderful woman, Debbie Fife, who had organized fund-raising events in New York City for twenty years. She said for us to be successful we would have to demonstrate that the David Lynch Foundation was a 'survival charity': that we were addressing a life-or-death concern that merited public support and private funding.

There are countless survival charities that do incredibly valuable work tackling the epidemics of cancer, heart disease, cystic fibrosis, HIV, and so on. What had been missing, I thought, was an organization that addresses with singular focus and expertise the crisis of toxic stress and trauma among vulnerable, at-risk populations.

We took Debbie Fife's advice. For several years, we

organized a series of national science conferences – led by top researchers, physicians, educators, and policy makers – to showcase the damaging effects of trauma on the brain and behaviour as well as the decades of research and clinical experience using TM to address this terrible epidemic. Fast-forward to today, and with the growing recognition of the horrors of trauma and the unique benefits of TM, our programmes are now in high demand in private and public schools, on military bases, and in prisons, women's shelters and HIV clinics. Yes, we are sometimes greeted with a bit of scepticism, but compared with even five years ago, there is very little hesitation or doubt. Thankfully.

Every day I read in the newspapers that mental health is increasingly at the forefront of debate in many countries – and for good reason. The elephant in the room is that no one really knows what to do about it. Do we medicate every child who may be a bully or is bullied? Do we continue to hand out cocktails of drugs to veterans with post-traumatic stress? While the medications are helpful for some, too many veterans are noncompliant; many don't like the numbness and disorientation they often feel medicated up, and so they refuse to take the drugs. Maybe they just want something better.

————————— • —————————

MEDITATIVE MOMENT
Charged at 100 Per cent Battery

Katy Perry has sold a zillion albums (give or take) and won countless awards for her music, is the first person in the world to have one hundred million Twitter followers, and has been at the top of the pop star universe for more than ten years – a century in normal human years. I taught Katy to meditate in 2010 when she was in India with comic actor Russell Brand, getting married. (The marriage didn't last, but the meditation did.) She is a kind, authentic and generous woman. Katy recently invited me to be a guest on her YouTube live webcast, which reached more than forty-nine million people. Katy calls her TM practice a 'game-changer,' one that allows her to bring her best to every situation, no matter how pressure packed and demanding.

Fundamentally, TM is the deepest rest I ever get. I dream a lot when I sleep, and this means I never fully get the rest that I need. Rest is so important for me and my vocals, because I operate best when I'm not tired. So I'll meditate before a show, which really helps. You would think I would fall asleep, but it actually leaves me feeling very reenergized.

Paris Fashion Week, I was out all night with friends,

and then I had to get up early for the runway shows. By the second show, I was a zombie. I meditated, and my friends thought the change in me was hysterical. Like I was Mary Poppins, 'Here I am! I'm wide awake!' They were like, 'Whoa, I wanna learn that.'

And I say, 'Do it!' TM training is my absolute favourite gift to give because it would be a shame not to share it with people who are suffering. I see their lives change, and I see how much joy and peace it brings them. I have a friend with PTSD who finally is able to sleep through the night.

But it's not just people who have such specific problems like that. We can all use it. We live in a world where personal time is obsolete. We are going to bed with our phones right here in front of our faces. We're never allowing our brain to rest anymore, which is so important for creativity, no matter what your job is. You have to 'install' a practice that helps your mind kind of reboot, just like your phone does sometimes. 'You have eighteen apps open; I'm gonna shut down on you.' In the same way, you need to unplug just for twenty minutes twice a day, and then you're good.

When I meditate, I physically feel a halo around my head, lighting up, sweeping the cobwebs, one by one, from around my brain. Thoughts will come and go, and it will be five minutes before I can get to that stillness. I go to this incredible place where I'm not even thinking anything. And yes I'm awake. It's so insane because I do feel like I'm using the most of my brain at that moment. I swear I can feel neural pathways opening up. Creatively, I get thoughts and ideas that maybe were buried at the bottom. They were dying to come out, but they were just covered by the dust of stress and fatigue.

That effect stays beyond the twenty minutes, and I can see it in my level of performance. I need to be able to live at my fullest capacity, and TM keeps me charged at 100 per cent battery.

———————— • ————————

The TM-based schools programme, also known as Consciousness-Based education (CBE), has been the flagship of the David Lynch Foundation since its launch in 2005. For two fifteen-minute periods twice a day, during each school day, the whole school is quiet. Students have a choice during that period: they can meditate or do something called 'silent, sustained reading,' or they can even nap. With their parents' encouragement and permission, most kids choose to meditate. The purpose of CBE is to give a short break, twice a day, dedicated not to jamming more facts and figures into their developing brains but to reducing stress and getting them ready to learn. And it works, as evidenced by the success of CBE programmes in schools for students of all ages all over the United States and around the world. Yes, Transcendental Meditation reduces stress and helps keep young people off drugs and out of trouble. But more than that, it wakes up the young person's brain, promotes learning readiness, and creates an optimal learning environment so students can develop their creative potential, assimilate knowledge, raise their academic achievement and be their best selves.

Dr George Rutherford was the first to see the value of Transcendental Meditation. Doc, as everyone calls him, is now in his late seventies. He has been a school principal and teacher for more than fifty-three years, running schools in some of the toughest, most crime-ridden areas in Washington, DC. He won't retire – he says he can't retire. He loves teaching and his kids so much. Doc is now the principal of the Ideal Academy Public Charter School, where he has instituted the Transcendental Meditation programme for all his students, teachers and administrators.

When I first met Doc in 1994, he was the principal of the Fletcher-Johnson Learning Center, a high school in the District's Ward 8, where murder rates were at their highest and where Doc held in his arms students with gun-shot wounds. Doc was the first public school principal in America to institute Transcendental Meditation schoolwide. I asked Doc at the time why he did it. He explained that a few months earlier, he had made a site visit to an amazing small school located in Fairfield, Iowa – 'in the middle of nowhere,' he said. What he saw at Maharishi School was hundreds of kids from age five to eighteen attend classes in Consciousness-Based education, with TM at the core of the otherwise traditional academic curriculum. And while the kids were learning a lot and excelling on academic test scores and in athletic competitions, what Doc noticed first and foremost was that they were happy. 'That's what I saw: happy kids,' Doc said. 'And I wanted my kids at Fletcher-Johnson to be happy just like those kids.' Now the Transcendental Meditation programme that Doc helped to start at Fletcher-Johnson has been incorporated into hundreds of schools with hundreds of thousands of kids around the world.

I remember the first time I visited Visitacion Valley Middle School in San Francisco. For a long time, it had been one of the worst-performing schools in the city. But now it had something going for it: principal Jim Dierke, a mustachioed, burly guy in his mid-fifties. He did not fit the stereotype of an educator who sees the potential of meditation in school.

But he, too, loved his kids. And he wanted to raise the academic achievement and promote a sense of wellbeing for the students living in a highly stressed environment. He'd tried everything to combat low attendance, violence and low performance.

Working with the Center for Wellness and Achievement in Education, a nonprofit sister organization to the David Lynch Foundation, Jim started a TM-based school programme. He began with a group of fourteen-year-old students. Compared with their peers who weren't offered Consciousness-Based education, the meditating students' suspensions fell by 45 per cent, and test scores jumped significantly relative to the others. Once TM was offered to the whole school, within four years the suspension rate was among the lowest in the city. In 2014, students at Visitacion Valley took the California Healthy Kids Survey of social and emotional health. They were asked to rank themselves with questions such as 'How much do you feel energetic right now?' and 'Since yesterday, how much have you felt grateful?' Even with all the issues outside its school walls, Visitacion Valley scored higher for happiness than any other school in San Francisco. Higher than even the most affluent schools where the kids have every advantage. Jim is retired now, but he got his wish for Visitacion Valley: happy kids given the opportunity to live up to their potential.

Joshua Aronson, a New York University psychologist and coauthor of The Social Animal, studies the social forces that shape academic success – everything from how poverty and prejudice undermine the confidence and learning of minority students and girls to the effects of student mindsets on their test scores. Joshua gained renown for developing interventions that boost achievement, but he told me that a visit to Visitacion Valley completely reoriented his focus to study the impact of meditation in schools.

'I saw children who were noticeably kinder and more peaceful toward one another as a result of the TM programme. I heard eleven-year-old kids speaking thoughtfully and with clarity about their feelings. I felt a sense of calm, support and humanity emanating from the kind of tough-looking "inner-city kids" who might easily scare you if you saw them on the street. Schools often bring out the worst in children – but Transcendental Meditation brings out the best,' Joshua told me. 'It's simply the most respectful, effective and elevating intervention I have ever seen. After a very short amount of time, you can feel the kids getting smarter, nicer and happier.'

TM works, and the data continue to bear it out. Research shows a highly significant 10 per cent increase in test scores. That was in a study of 189 students aged between twelve and thirteen who were below the baseline proficiency level in maths and English using the California Standards Tests. TM was taught and practised in the school as it continued with the school's standard curriculum and instruction. At three months, the meditating students improved at least one performance level in maths and English compared with controls.[5]

In another study, forty-five African American students aged fifteen to eighteen were assigned randomly to either a Transcendental Meditation group or a control group of students who studied the basics of good health. The meditation group engaged in fifteen-minute sessions at home and at school each day for four months. The control group was given fifteen-minute sessions of health education at school each day for four months. The results were clear even before the next academic exam: there was an obvious, significant reduction in negative school behaviours, with decreases in absenteeism, school rule infractions and suspension days.[6]

Naturally, TM helps teachers too. Look at a recent study of forty secondary school teachers and support staffers at the Bennington School in Vermont, a therapeutic school for children with behavioural problems. After four months, the faculty and staff showed significant reductions in stress and burnout.[7]

Educators also remember why they wanted to become educators in the first place. Educators such as Michael Barakat. I met Michael a few years ago when I moderated a panel discussion on the TM programme for two hundred school principals and other administrators in New York. Afterward, I stuck around for questions when this tall, youthful-looking man in his midthirties came up.

'We're gonna do this,' he said.

Now, I confess I was in Q&A mode, so I was just anticipating questions or concerns. 'Oh, great,' I said. 'I'm glad you're interested.'

'Oh no,' he said. 'You misunderstand. We're going to do this. What are the next steps?'

I never should have underestimated Michael Barakat, principal of the Bronx High School for Law and Community Service. I later found out that he started there as principal in 2010, taking on a failing school with a D rating and just points way from an F. Only 47 per cent of the students were graduating in four years. 'It was made very clear,' Principal Barakat told me, 'that if we didn't turn the school around, it would be closed.'

Principal Barakat is achievement focused and data driven. The first thing he did was the obvious: he focused on academics. 'I said, "If I can change the name of the school to 'Reading, Writing and Arithmetic,' I would,"' he recalled. 'It was a severe first year, but people were not graduating. That's what people are supposed to do from a high school; they are supposed to graduate.'

The first year of focus reset the system, and by 2015, he had raised the graduation rate from 47 per cent to 73 per cent, even before implementing Transcendental Meditation. 'I have so many students working their tails off,' he said, 'to do everything in their power to achieve the ever-increasing goals that are set for them.'

And they are doing this as they face struggles at home. 'My school is above eighty-five per cent Title I, meaning the students get free or reduced lunch because their household incomes are below the poverty level,' he said. 'So they have a certain set of socioeconomic disadvantages.'

When Principal Barakat heard about Transcendental Meditation, he says he knew it at least deserved a shot. Before bringing the programme to his school, he put it to the teachers for a vote. 'I wanted a majority,' he said. 'To make it work, we had to reduce the students' lunch period from fifty minutes to thirty-five minutes each day and take five minutes off each class period to get the goal of eighteen minutes of meditation in the morning before second period and eighteen minutes after seventh period.' (There are nine periods in a day at Bronx High School for Law and Community Service.)

Some teachers expressed concern that a more compressed class schedule would lead to lower student achievement. 'In an age of high-stakes testing and accountability,' he said, 'I understand that.' He negotiated the schedule change with the teachers' union. Principal Barakat was excited with the development but, he said, he was anticipating what he called 'a PR nightmare' when he brought it to students and parents. What actually happened was a surprise.

'Out of the four hundred and twenty kids at the school, I had only two parents who had differences,' he said. 'So we just set up an alternative where those two students would go help in the main office during the meditation period.'

The programme started on the first day of school in September 2015, and he watched the rollout closely. 'My main question was: For the five minutes that we took off of each class period to make this happen, did we gain ten minutes of attention? Did we gain ten minutes of ability to actually be *heard* by a student?'

It seemed to be working soon after the start. 'It's funny, because we were sitting around racking our brains about what metrics we would use to measure this as a success or failure,' explained Principal Barakat. 'Because TM is such a qualitative experience, how could we quantify it?'

A veteran teacher volunteered an observation. 'Students don't fall asleep in class anymore,' she said. 'I always had to say to students, especially toward the end of the day, "Come on, stay awake, it's just a little bit longer."'

The teachers realized they'd all seen that marked difference. The kids were showing the 'restful alertness' that is a hallmark of TM. More pointedly, the teachers soon saw better test scores and, by the end of one year with the programme, a jump in the graduation rate. 'Our rate went up five points, and it's now above seventy-eight per cent,' Principal Barakat told me with deserved pride. 'The citywide and statewide averages fluctuate, but they're always somewhere in the lower to mid-sixties. To me, that's the ultimate metric because it's the culmination of *all* of our other metrics. It all goes to graduation rates.'

There was also what he heard privately from students. The principal had always had a safe school with good kids, but he knew there were conflicts at home. 'Someone told me she was about to have a fight with her mum and decided to meditate instead,' said Principal Barakat.

Just as in other Consciousness-Based education schools across the country, the faculty of Bronx High School for Law and Community Service seemed to benefit along with the kids. When the superintendent came in, as Principal Barakat put it, for a routine 'white-glove' inspection, people weren't as nervous and freaked out as they had been in the past. They were confident and excited to talk about the school. 'The urgency has not left,' he said, 'but the panic about trying to do something that can seem mathematically impossible given budgets and expectations – that's gone. That difference is palpable.'

Principal Barakat sees the potential to help kids of all socioeconomic levels. 'Having spoken to colleagues on the other side of the coin, there are tremendous pressures on students coming from what we would call an advantaged background,' he said. 'So in no way am I saying that only poor, under-represented students need to meditate. Quite the contrary. I think we are doing a disservice to all our students by sticking to an arcane curriculum that does not teach life skills. And I consider Transcendental Meditation to be a basic life skill.'

The University of Chicago Crime and Urban Education Labs are tackling the epidemic of youth violence. Each year, roughly fifty thousand people are murdered worldwide, and while mortality rates from almost every other leading cause of death have declined dramatically in the last century, current homicide rates in America are about the same as they were in 1900. The Crime Lab uses science – harnessing the power of administrative data through randomized, controlled studies – to learn about innovative and effective ways to reduce violence. This research helps inform policy makers, academics, funders and practitioners of what works, for whom, and why, so that every dollar spent to curb violence is spent wisely.

In its search for solutions, in 2015 the Crime Lab put out a request for proposals for innovative programmes and ideas to reduce youth violence through the Chicago Design Competition.

'It's where we crowdsource the best ideas,' says John Wolf, senior programme manager at the Crime Lab. 'We ask people on the front lines, who are doing the work, what are the *best* ideas for tackling this problem?'

More than 220 organizations competed for the funding, including the David Lynch Foundation. The Crime Lab, in partnership with the Pritzker Pucker Family Foundation and the MacArthur Foundation, selected the David Lynch Foundation as one of three winners, and awarded the DLF office in Chicago nearly $300,000 to study the effects of Transcendental Meditation in two schools in distressed neighbourhoods in Chicago.

'I had some scepticism when we initially looked at the programme,' John Wolf told me. 'We're gonna have high school students do what? Are they really going to want to do that every day? We knew there was promising data coming out of schools in San Francisco, but there was some thought of, "Okay that's San Francisco ..." But could this actually be effective in Chicago? We decided to give the David Lynch Foundation a year to prove it could.'

The Chicago Public Schools system helped the Crime Lab choose the two schools for the pilot programme. At the time of the first interim report in December 2015, the programme had been implemented at Amundsen High and Gage Park High. And the results were already showing. At Gage Park, an overwhelming majority of students practising TM said they were feeling less stressed and calmer. And at Amundsen, nearly all the meditating students reported feeling less stress as well as less anxiety with better sleep habits. They also said they were better able to handle the pressures of heavy academic workloads.

'After a year of the programme, we interviewed students, and talked to teachers and administrators,' John Wolf continued. 'The enthusiasm of the administrative staff at both Gage Park and Amundsen, as well as their claims of improved conduct among students in the programme, is promising.' The full-scale research project will be able to determine whether the positive changes that the administrators attributed to Transcendental Meditation are caused by the programme.

The TM schools programme has received glowing reports. One school in particular chose a group of students who historically had a lot of mental health issues because of the track they are on academically and the pressures they face. The school reported that there were zero official mental health reports out of the group of sixty students in the programme.

After gathering all the information from the pilot programme, the Crime Lab increased its grant by nearly $1 million in 2016 so that the programme could be offered in three more schools, again in some of the toughest areas of the city. The three schools selected by the Chicago Public School system and the Crime Lab are in the south and west of the city, historically its most disadvantaged and violent areas.

The study has school classes randomized where every student in a class either meditates or doesn't meditate but does another quiet activity. The Crime Lab is comparing outcomes between the two groups in regard to attendance, suspensions, grades, standardized test scores and arrests.

John Wolf told me that through focus groups conducted at both pilot schools, students reported benefits in four main areas: (1) sleep, (2) self-awareness and self-control, (3) ability to focus, and (4) mood, sharing that they felt calmer and better able to cope with stress both in and outside of school. This study confirmed that the programme could be implemented with fidelity, and suggested encouraging avenues along which meditation impacts student health.

John said that he finds the data so promising that the

Crime Lab is working to secure the additional funds to bring the programme to several thousand more students in Chicago as well as New York City public schools in the next few years.

I've thrown a lot of data about Transcendental Meditation at you because I get enthusiastic about the outcomes. But there is one story that is more powerful than any statistic. A couple of years back, I got a call from Ben, a teacher at an urban secondary school in a tough neighbourhood. The school had recently begun a programme, offering TM on a voluntary basis to all its students, faculty and staff. Ben wanted to tell me about one of his students, an eleven-year-old whom I will call Charlene.

At Ben's school, each student has to be in his or her seat before the first period class bell rings to be able to meditate with the class. If students are late, they have to meditate out in the hall. Not bad, of course, but the kids like to meditate together.

'It was three minutes after the class bell rang, and Charlene burst through the door,' Ben said.

She sat down with a crash at her desk, and Ben waited a moment before walking softly over to her. 'I told her the bell had rung, and she'd have to do her meditation in the hall,' he said. When Charlene stood to leave, Ben noticed that she had dark-red paint splattered over part of her dress.

'I told her we needed to call her mum and ask for a change of clothes,' Ben said. 'And she just burst into tears. And through the sobs, she whispered, "It's blood."'

Charlene had been standing next to her uncle at a bus stop near the school when a bullet in a drive-by shooting struck him. It was her uncle's blood on her dress. Panicked, she had nowhere safe to run – except to school, where she could meditate. School was her sole safe haven. Not home, not a friend's house, but school. Schools, which have become breeding grounds for drugs, violence and crime, are transformed through Transcendental Meditation.

———————— · ————————

MEDITATIVE MOMENT
A Parallel Stream of Consciousness

Russell Brand had been a heroin addict for more than fourteen years, and he was five years clean from drugs and alcohol when I met him. He'd reached out because he was producing a documentary on his life's journey and was interested in learning to meditate as part of the project. I mentioned this to a friend. 'Be careful,' she said. 'He's a very funny guy, but see if he'll take you seriously.'

Russell was staying at the Soho House in New York. We met in the restaurant. He's easy to spot, so I waved to him, and he came over and put his face about three inches from mine, staring me right in the eye.

'Are you going to teach me Transcendental Meditation?'

'It depends on if you have the time,' I said.

His face completely softened, and he gave the look of someone truly open and ready.

'I've been searching for the experience of timeless my whole life,' he said. 'I have as much time as you want.'

I taught Russell about two weeks later, and we have remained close friends since. That was almost seven years ago.

The idea of meditation was challenging because I had this initial response, which now I recognize is a quite clichéd one: 'I don't know if I'll be able to meditate because my mind is so busy and I'm always thinking.' But it's part of my life now. I've not been able to say, 'I never missed a session,' but I've been good with it. It's become part of my identity.

I would argue that even addiction such as I had was its own form of spiritual quest. It's a sense of disease, unease and dissatisfaction that led me to chemical dependency. Since meditating regularly, the way I see the world and what I want for myself has changed. I always have to be mindful and point out that it's not, 'Oh yeah, I used to be that crazy drug addict and womanizer, and now I'm just basically sitting around with a blanket wrapped around me looking at a cool, calm lake thinking George Harrison lyrics.' I'm not. I've still got desire in me. Fear. Lust. I'm full of human flesh-based stuff, but what's happened is that a neglected aspect of me has been awoken and cultivated through this meditative practice.

Meditation for me is a continual parallel stream of consciousness, ever present, usually ignored, that I can step into at any time.

Often I like to engage in illusion and self-deception: 'It's fine to take drugs,' 'I deserve to be famous,' or 'Sex and money are great.' But beneath these temporal and sensory distractions, the limitless flow abides. Like space, like time, misunderstood due to its boundless nature.

Without meditation, we are worse than apes. Apes that can speak and are aware of their apeness. There ain't enough bananas in the world for me to deal with that.

———————— • ————————

I must add a personal note here that Russell, as well as the other artists and performers whom I have included in these pages, have been incredibly generous with their time and resources. Russell, who is the author of the bestseller *Recovery: Freedom From Our Addictions*, is working with the David Lynch Foundation to bring the Transcendental Meditation technique to adults and teens who are battling substance use disorder of all types. He is helping to save lives.

Martin G. is a 32-year-old former addict from Glasgow, Scotland, who suffered through long years of anxiety, depression, addiction, suicide attempts and all-consuming feelings of hopelessness. He is, of course, not alone. In every country the numbers are rising. And terribly, we all know someone who has been there, or is there now. Maybe someone in your family is suffering, or you may have felt that way yourself. Martin started meditating six years ago after hearing Howard Stern talk about his 50-year practice of TM on Howard's SiriusXM radio show. Martin says meditating changed his life. I asked him why he decided to learn.

'Desperation,' Martin replied immediately. 'I was anxious and depressed. I had an addiction to valium, codeine and alcohol, and I had recently gotten sober after a suicide attempt. I was looking for something to replace the alcohol and drugs because my anxiety and depression only increased after I stopped self-medicating. I had been prescribed lithium plus an antidepressant by a psychiatrist but the drugs had a minimal effect – mostly numbness. I stopped going outside because I couldn't leave my flat without having a panic attack. To kill all those hours in my flat I started listening to Howard Stern on the radio, and that's when I first heard about TM. I got intrigued and I decided to learn. That was nearly six years ago – and after just three years of regular meditation I was able to stop taking the lithium and anti-depressants the doctor prescribed. It was hard coming off the medication. My moods and thoughts were all over the place. But thanks to the technique, I finally had a tool to process my feelings instead of just avoiding them.

'Over time, my diet changed. I became aware that I was mindlessly stuffing garbage into my face every time I felt a negative emotion or twinge of anxiety.

'Plus, over time my sleeping, waking and eating times have become consistent – and I've added exercise to my daily routine.

'Finally, being around people has never been easy for me. And while I still find social situations difficult, my awareness during those times is so different now. I'm able to step outside of myself and see the bigger picture instead of just reacting. This has made my relationships with others so much better,' says Martin, who is now attending evening writing courses while looking for work. 'My life has changed,' he says.

*   *   *

I pride myself in thinking big with our work. I thought I had done that. And then I learned I needed to think even bigger.

A couple of years ago, I was meeting with some civic and community leaders in Newark, New Jersey, to develop a large research protocol for the schools that would provide the meditation to all the students, teachers, administrators and parents in the city who wanted to learn. The study would investigate the impact of TM on stress, health, behaviour, and academic performance – as well as teacher burnout, absenteeism and school district health costs.

We completed the plan, and I went to speak to Richard, who headed up a large hedge fund in Midtown Manhattan, to discuss possible financial support. I quite proudly plunked the thick proposal on his desk and announced that we had a plan to address the damaging influence of trauma and stress on education in Newark. He glanced at the title page with 'Newark' emblazoned across the top, and pushed the papers aside.

'Do you believe,' Richard asked, 'that trauma is a major health crisis among the young?'

'Yes,' I said.

'Do you believe that TM can help address that problem?'

'Uh, yes, I do,' I said as politely as I could, to hide my impatience. 'That's the reason for the proposal.'

'Then why are you thinking so small? Why a plan just for kids in Newark? Why aren't you thinking for every child in America – in fact, the world? If you came to me seventy years ago with a proposal to cure childhood polio,' Richard said, 'would you have shown me a plan that would help only the kids in Newark? Of course not. Come back with a bigger plan.'

He was, of course, right. When it comes to a new medicine that has been shown to effectively address a terrible epidemic, the delivery strategy is global, never just local.

*   *   *

For the first ten years of the David Lynch Foundation, we focused on implementing programmes and evaluating the outcomes when TM was introduced in entire schools, veterans' service organizations, women's shelters, treatment programmes for substance use disorders, juvenile justice centres, HIV clinics – as well as Fortune 100 companies, professional athletic teams, military bases and other governmental organizations. And so on.

The data is quite heartening and quite compelling.

Now, in our second decade, our focus has naturally shifted to scalability. How can we bring the benefits of meditation to as many people as possible? To this end, we are working with a bipartisan group of members of Congress and leaders of government agencies to secure support for these programmes (and other innovative, evidence-based programmes that work) as well as the UN, NGOs and other organizations so they can be offered on a large scale. At the same time, we are working with medical schools and research institutions to evaluate the impact of these initiatives, including for cost savings. And we continue to partner with a growing number of foundations and philanthropists to expand our initiatives right now.

Bridgewater Associates founder Ray Dalio and his wife, Barbara, have given me keen insight into the minds of true benefactors. It comes down to the lesson we hopefully all learn from our parents or mentors growing up. 'When you have it to give, give.' Ray has personally helped to underwrite the cost of many hundreds of people in his company to learn to meditate, and he and Barbara have helped many thousands of others learn TM through their generous donations to the David Lynch Foundation.

'I started with nothing,' Ray said, 'and I have been very lucky to live in a country that has provided me with lots of opportunity, and I happen to be in a career that led me to make a lot of money.

'I was faced with the question of "What should I do with that money before I die?"' he said. 'I don't want to give a lot of money to my kids, because the thing that I want them to have more than anything is strength, and that comes from struggling. At the same time, I get a tremendous kick out of having a big impact on people and causes where the marginal impact of the money I am providing is huge. Obviously, it seems the sensible and exciting thing to do.

'My family members have experienced the same benefits from TM as I have. So how could we not support giving TM to stressed at-risk students in under-served schools and veterans who suffer the nightmare of post-traumatic stress?'

———————— • ————————

MEDITATIVE MOMENT
Back to My Most Natural State

Lena Dunham, creator of the groundbreaking HBO series Girls *and bestselling author, has been meditating since she was nine years old. Her parents meditated, and Lena says her mother, artist Laurie Simmons, brought her to a TM teacher to help her with what looked like the beginning of obsessive-compulsive disorder, or OCD. I was fortunate to give Lena a refresher course in TM as she was finishing up her work on Girls. She talked to me about TM's impact on her creative process – and how it helps her get out of her own way.*

At the most root level, what meditation does for me is bring me back to my most natural state and remind me what my value is in the world. There's all the stuff that is set up in the world to distract us from our most basic self and our most basic instinct. It's so easy to get caught up in challenges and ambition, and there's so much fear and anxiety that accompany modern life. For me, meditation is the thing that shows me what we all are. It sounds so mystical, but it's actually so basic.

A lot of people think – and I used to be one of these people – that they're creative because they're suffering. When really, that is actually so antithetical to making things that you're proud of. There are so many people who are caught up in the idea that if they're happy in their family life, or if they're in love, or if they aren't drinking themselves into oblivion every night, that somehow the magical thing that allows them to make art is going to disappear. I know I fell victim to that idea. Now I realize I've actually been creating *in spite* of all that, not because of it.

It's funny, when I mention meditation, people's eyes

kind of light up because there's all these people who are clearly looking for anything that will give them superhuman productivity and power. So initially what attracts them to meditation is their sort of baser instincts, but once they do it, they find these other things coming to light. They go in saying, 'I want to be able to sleep less, make more money and have it all.' Now they're meditating, and suddenly they have an insight into their other behaviours that they didn't have otherwise.

I was at the airport flipping through some trashy magazine waiting for my flight, and I saw this article saying, 'Try the technique all the stars are doing,' and then there was a description of Transcendental Meditation. I guess whatever has to happen to get meditation out into the world, but it's so funny when TM is on the same page as diet tips!

_____ . _____

As I have learned to think bigger, people often ask me what I would like to see happen with TM in America and the world.

I would like everyone to know what the technique is and to have access to it if they would like to learn – either through a TM centre in their community or through their company, school, or university. Or through a community health centre, veterans' service organization, and so forth. For many people with an interest, however, time can be a confounding issue: time to find out about it, time to be instructed, time to meditate. Fortunately, the world is changing, and more businesses now have meditation rooms along with gyms, and schoolteachers are able to use their faculty lounges for afternoon meditations. Ten years ago, that might have sounded ludicrous, but no more, because we ignore the deadly ramifications of stress at our own peril. Making it easy for employees to take a few minutes out of a busy day to meditate makes good sense for health, productivity and the bottom line.

For those people for whom money is tight, the non-profit TM organizations in the UK and Australia are generous, providing grants, scholarships and loans to help people in financial need whenever funds are available. Work is also under way with employee assistance programmes, insurance providers and government agencies to provide coverage for the TM course fee – just as these agencies would with any other evidence-based treatment.

And for people who suffer from trauma and toxic stress and who have no access to funds, the David Lynch Foundation continues to raise support from corporations, foundations and philanthropists so we can provide scholarships for the many millions of people who are desperate to learn.

This is our strategy, and the response has been excellent. Soon everyone who wants to learn how to meditate will be able to do so. That was Maharishi's goal back in 1958 when he first started teaching TM – and that is the same goal today.

————————— • —————————

MEDITATIVE MOMENT
Opening the Door for Stillness and Strength

For Dr Tony Nader the ravages of war were not something he saw in movies or read about in books. He saw it firsthand. Born and raised in Lebanon, he attended medical school in Beirut during some of the bloodiest periods of the 15-year Lebanese Civil War. He earned his medical degree from American University there and then moved to the United States, where he attended MIT and earned a Ph.D. in brain and cognitive science. He also served as clinical and research fellow in neurology at the Massachusetts General Hospital–Harvard Medical School and the assistant director of the Clinical Research Center at MIT.

Dr Nader first met Maharishi in 1979 at MIT. Over decades, a unique, trusted mentor–apprentice relationship developed. Before Maharishi passed in 2008, he asked Dr Nader to oversee the entire global TM organization.

I was studying pre-med at American University in Beirut in 1975 at the start of the civil war. There were shootings and bombs; people getting kidnapped because of their religion. Sometimes, for months at a time, I couldn't travel from the university across the city to visit my parents because there was so much violence.

During those days, I was searching for meaning amidst the destruction, looking for a way to meditate. I tried a concentration technique for a little while and I also did some breathing exercises. But I didn't get anywhere. Then I heard about Transcendental Meditation from a friend and I decided to try it out. Right away, I experienced something I had been seeking for a long time: transcendence – a deep inner calm, a deep inner bliss and a great expansion of awareness. It was tremendously satisfying. I had more energy and clarity to study better, to be more focused and accomplish more. Most important, TM helped me remain settled inside even though I was surrounded by fear and loss and violence. I opened a TM club at American University and I got my family and friends to learn to meditate as well.

Living in a war zone, I had a desire to understand exactly what happens in the minds of people that would make them want to fight. I specialized in psychiatry in medical school and that gave me some insight but not enough. I became a TM teacher after I completed medical school and then I entered a Ph.D. programme in neuroscience at MIT. I wanted to better understand the science of TM and the brain so I could do more than just treat a disease but really improve a person's health, really develop his or her creative potential. Not just in limited ways from the chemical-neurophysiological level, but from the unlimited level of the human mind as well. I conducted research on neurochemistry, neuroendocrinology and the relationship between diet, age and behaviour and neurotransmitter and hormonal activity, and on the role of neurotransmitter precursors in medicine.

When I met Maharishi at MIT, it was the beginning of what I can best describe as an apprenticeship that lasted decades. I learned from Maharishi the deep connections between the ancient Vedic science of consciousness and the form and function of the human brain and physiology. I travelled all over the world and spoke with leaders in government, medicine, education, business and defence about the science of consciousness. Over time, Maharishi gave me more and more responsibility for the knowledge and the administration of the global TM organization. It was nothing I ever imagined coming my way.

People often ask me about Maharishi. I think Maharishi's achievements speak best for who he was. I believe history will recognize Maharishi as the foremost scientist of consciousness, the one who revived the simplicity and naturalness of Transcendental Meditation. He opened the door for everyone – no matter his or her education, nationality, or religion – to experience real inner stillnesss, transcendence, and to develop real inner strength, higher states of consciousness. This has been Maharishi's great contribution to the field of science, to the study of human consciousness, and to life.

———————— • ————————

A reporter from the Associated Press was interviewing Maharishi for a feature story about the fiftieth anniversary of his TM organization back in June 2007. I had taught the reporter to meditate a few days before and had the opportunity to sit in on the conversation. After a series of almost perfunctory questions, the reporter asked Maharishi about his 'overly optimistic view' of the impact of meditation on people suffering from a host of traumas and stress-related disorders. Such suffering had existed for centuries, the reporter said, and was not going away anytime soon. How, then, could Maharishi be so hopeful?

Maharishi thought for a minute, nodded, and said, 'Darkness is just the absence of light. Turn on the light, and the darkness disappears. You can have a room that has been in darkness for one day, and you can have a room that has been in darkness for a thousand years. When you turn on a light in each room, the darkness disappears just as fast. Like that is the impact of Transcendental Meditation in the life of the individual and, by extension, the whole of society.'

I am incredibly positive about what TM can do for you and for our larger world. Mainly because I have experienced it firsthand for nearly fifty years and because I have seen its dramatic impact in the lives of thousands of people I have personally taught, some of whom live in the darkest, most violent, most dire conditions imaginable.

Should you choose to learn to meditate, I offer my full support and the full support of every other TM teacher in the world as you begin this journey to experience and express the boundless reservoir of creativity and intelligence that lies within you. It's such a simple thing, but it's also incredibly powerful. Enjoy.

ACKNOWLEDGEMENTS

I am first and foremost grateful to Maharishi Mahesh Yogi for making available to everyone, in the simplest possible way, this most natural technique for accessing the inner field of stillness, which is the basis of real health, happiness and success in life. I am thankful to Dr Tony Nader for shouldering with exceptional wisdom, compassion, patience and strength the global responsibility for teaching Transcendental Meditation in 120 countries since Maharishi's passing in 2008; to Dr John Hagelin, for his wise and steady stewardship in guiding the teaching of TM in hundreds of centres throughout the United States; to Dr Bevan Morris for his focused, decades-long dedication to promoting and safeguarding the integrity and power of the TM technique now and for the future; to David Lynch, for creating the David Lynch Foundation for Consciousness-Based Education and World Peace in his name and for his tireless efforts around the world to bring this meditation to millions of people; to Dr Norman Rosenthal, for his close friendship and scientific acumen that helped inform the writing of this book and, truly, to the thousands of teachers of Transcendental Meditation for everything you do, every day, to make a better world.

To Ray and Barbara Dalio, Devon and Jane Dalio, Paul and Kristina and Christopher and Kai Dalio, Matt Dalio, and Mark Dalio – there are simply no words to express how deeply I love and appreciate you all – for who you are and all you do.

My heartfelt thanks continue with enthusiasm. To Albert Lee, my visionary, persevering and always accommodating agent and friend at Aevitas Creative, who first caught the idea that I should write a book and encouraged me every step of the way to make it happen; to Kevin O'Leary, my incredibly smart, empathic and soulful collaborator for your constant support, wise direction and excellent wordsmithery in carrying this book from pre-inception to completion; and at Simon & Schuster, to president and publisher Jon Karp, for trusting and green-lighting this project; to Jofie Ferrari-Adler, my wise, patient and always supportive editor, as well as his assistant Julianna Haubner; to Richard Rhorer, Cary Goldstein, Stephen Bedford and the whole publicity and marketing team for your energetic and tireless dedication to the book; to art director Alison Forner, interior designer Carly Loman, copyeditor Phil Bashe, and director of copyediting Navorn Johnson, for making me look as good as possible; and at Simon & Schuster UK, to my wonderful editor Claudia Connal, PR manager Gemma Conley-Smith, and marketing executive Amy Fulwood for your energy, vision and support.

This book is the fruit of the hard work and dedication of everyone in the David Lynch Foundation and TM organizations worldwide. My heartfelt thanks to David Lynch Foundation Board members (past and present) Jeffrey and Rona Abramson, Vincent Argiro, Mark Axelowitz, Ramani Ayer, Jill Black, David Ford, Aryn Grossman, Bob Jones, Joni Kimberlin, Nigol Koulajian, Jennifer Leahy, Bud Liebler, Richard Creighton and Jane Ottenberg, Joanna Plafsky, Barry Scherr, Orin Snyder and Bruce Wilpon.

To the DLF executive team Rena Boone, Chris and Julia Busch, Salma Choudhury-Muro, Ina Rose Clark, Jon Haseltine, Raji Kalra, Lynn Kaplan, Mario Orsatti and Linda Mainquist, Deirdre Parsons, Rece Reid and Maximus, and Fredda Plesser and Andy Turtel.

To my fellow TM teachers, team members and friends

whose support for the work has meant everything to me, including Steve Abrams, Lindsey Adelman, Sagen Albert, Reza Ali, Dr Jose Luis Alvarez Roset, Brecon Anastasio, Lisa Angrame, Shane and Louise Anselmi, Kevin Ashley, Austin Ayer, David and Alatia Bach, Dr Rodgers and Candace Badgett, Michael Barile, Ron Barnett, Dusty Baxley, Larry and Maria Baum, Richard Beall, Sarah Rose Belok, Alexander Berg, Lucy Clare Beuchert, Sai Bhatnagar, Buddy Biancalana, Chuck Bliziotis, Jared and Mayte Bluestein, Cindy Johnson-Boka, Carole Bonhomme, Preston Boulton, Natane Boudreau, Joe Boxerman; Barbara, Laura, and Mabel Brand; Kingsley and Leslie Brooks, Mark Bunn, Michael and Pegi Busch, Rebecca Busch, Matt Butler, Marilyn Caufield, Howard Chancellor, Greg Chapman, Dr Barry Charles, Ken Chawkin, Michael Kubin and Nancy Chemtob, Jonathan Cohen, Joshua Cohen, Blaze Compton, Kathy Connor, Kevin Cook, Sara Costello, Candy Crowley, Elliot Cuker, Rachel Cutler, Bob Daniels, Rafael David, Martin Davy, Vin DeCrescenzo, Dr Michael and Dr Susie Dillbeck, Peter Dodge, Patti Donatella, Dean Draznin, Christina Drossakis, Donnie and Martha Durham, Michael and Dina Dwyer, Rob Eberley, Nian Fish, Cindy Feinberg, Becky Fleming, Naomi Foner, Lisa Fox, Fatima Franco, Donielle Freeberg, Elizabeth Freund,

Adam Friedman, Stuart Friedman, Ra Frye, Yanira Funes, Bill Goldstein, Liz Goldwyn, Denny Goodman, Dr Jamie and Ann Grant, Fred and Shelley Gratzon, Yael Greenberg, Elliot Groffman, Erin Groman, Roger and Katie Grose, Desiree Gruber, Sandy Haas, Kara Hagelin, Lee Hagelin, Chas Hall, Hayley Hanna, Shepley Hansen, Dave and Dee Hardin, Jessica W. Harris, the Harrison family, Heather Hartnett, Laurie Heilman, Percilla Herrera, Leonard and Penny Hintz, David Hirsch, Stephanie Hirsch, Richard Hobbs, Harbour Hodder, Mitch Horowitz, Ellen Akst Jones, Ellen Karis, Jack Davies and Kay Kendall, Kevin Kimberlin, Maddy Koch, Jayme Koszyn, Carl Kuehner, Oscar Jackman, Genevieve Jarvis, Jerry and Debby Jarvis, Sam Johnson, Craig Kallman, Drew and Rachel Katz, Sam and Melody Katz, Maddy Koch, Gary Korf, Michael Lackman, Peter Lamoureux, Fred and Seen Landman, Carol Lawrence, Tina Le, Lyle Lederer, the Lennon family, Nancy Liebler, Donovan and Linda Leitch, Erin Levi, David and Simone Levinson; Toby, Sam, and Eli Lieb; Nick Linnen, George and Nitzia Logothetis, Aurora Lopez, Mike Love, Jennifer, Austin, Riley, and Lula Lynch; Wesley Lyons, Kelly Malloy, Lucy Margan, Bob and Carol Markowitz, Erik Martin, Sunita Martin, Raisa Martinez, Scott and Suna Maslin, Claudia Mason, Dan McCarroll, the McCartney family,

Kathleen McKay, Louisa Merino, Gabrielle Messinger, Steven Meyer, Bob Miller, Noriko Miyakawa, Jonathon Mize, Shujaa and Jessie Mjasiri, Bianca Monda, Celio Mondjane, Buck and Cathy Montgomery; Cody Montgomery; Ian, Leila, Dil (Hurlin), and Lyra Montgomery; Brianna Moriarty, Angie Morteo, Daron and Laura Dawn Murphy, Ed Murphy, Maina Mwangi, Hilla Narov, Ariel Nathanson, Adam Nathel, Muriel Nellis, Donna Nelson, Cara Nielsen, Lincoln and June Norton, Lindsay Oliver, Sally Ourieff, Carol Palma, Sasha Parmasad, Neil Patterson, Craig Pearson, Antwan Penn, Jane Roman Pitt, Robert Mulhall and Joanna Pitt, Elijah Alexander, Jesse, Aviva, Annalise, and Micah Pitt; Joshua Pittman, Joe and Susan Plumeri, Stacy Bash-Polley, Adam Pressman, Ann Purcell, Carolyn Rafaelian, Mindy Ramaker, Gaile Ramey, Brendan Reape, Dr Brian Rees, Donald Revolinski, Elizabeth Rice-Arnold, Kate Richard, Steve Richter, Craig Ridgley, Jack and Vicki Rovner, Dennis Rowe, Dr Steve and Karen Rubin, Jonathan Rudney, Sheri Salata, Bill Sands, Monica Sanny, Heidi Schecter, Ed and Judy Schloeman, Sylvia Schmidt, Adrienne Schoenfeld, Mark Schoenfeld, Eric Schwartz, Olivia Shepherd, Sarah Sica, Jack and Shirley Silver, Dr Sean Slifer, Brian Smith, Cliff and Barbara Sobel, Scott and Lori Sobel, Andy Sommers, Barry Sommers, George Verschoor and Gayle Spitz, Iseo Squaranti, Sheila Stamps, the Starr family, Dr Suzanne Steinbaum, Zach Sternberg, Michael Sternfeld, Doug Stewart, Emily Stofle, Cheryl Stone, Kennidy Stood, David and Kathy Streid, Michael Sullivan, Sabrina Sutherland, Peter and Susie Swan, Katie Tagarello, Lincoln Taggert, Chandrika Tandon, Debbie Thompson, Mike Tompkins, Peter Trivelas, Anna Unger, Velky Valentin, Laurent Valosek, Abdiel Vivancos, Charlie and Lauran Walk, Scott Walker, Dr Peter Warburton, Ruby Warrington, Pamela Weiner, Mike Weisensee, Mark Williams, Grant Wilson, Isaac Winkler, Zola Winley, Jerry Yellin, Steve Yellin, Nahshon Yisrael, Norman Zierold, Adam Zipper, Dave Zobeck, and to my other dear friends and fellow travellers at the David Lynch Foundation and the TM organizations worldwide.

Most especially, to my beloved parents, Merall and Susan; siblings Ellen, Bill, Tom and Scott; and nephews Jonny Cook and Michael and Rachel Cook and their children Hazel and April – to all of you, for your constant, unimaginable, and life-sustaining love and support. All of this happened because of you. In truth, this is your book.

NOTES

Introduction

1. Jean-Pierre Brun, 'Work-Related Stress: Scientific Evidence-Base of Risk Factors, Prevention and Costs' (presentation, World Health Organization, March 2007); Judy Martin. 'Stress at Work Is Bunk for Business,' *Forbes* online, last modified 2 August 2012.

2. Katie Allen, 'Stress Now Commonest Cause of Long-Term Sick Leave – Report,' *Guardian* online, last modified 4 October 2011.

3. Etsuro Totsuka and Toshio Ueyanag, 'Prevention of Death from Overwork and Remedies for Its Victims,' National Defense Counsel for Victims of Karoshi, http://karoshi.jp/english/overwork1.html; 'Case Study – Karoshi: Death from Overwork,'

International Labour Organisation online, last modified 23 April 2013, www.ilo.org/safework/info/publications/WCMS_211571/lang – en/index.htm.

4. Frederick Travis and Jonathan Shear, 'Focused attention, open monitoring and automatic self-transcending: Categories to organize meditations from Vedic, Buddhist and Chinese traditions,' *Consciousness and Cognition* 19 (December 2010): 1110–19.

5. J. Hagelin et al., 'A Self-Referral Default Brain State: Patterns of Coherence, Power and eLORETA Sources During Eyes-Closed Rest and the Transcendental Meditation Practice', *Cognitive Processes*, 11 (1), 21–30.

PILLAR ONE
A Working Definition

1. Frederick Travis and Niyazi Parim, 'Default Mode Network Activation and Transcendental Meditation Practice: Focused Attention or Automatic Self-Transcending?', *Brain and Cognition* 111 (February 2017): 86–94, http://dx.doi.org/10.1016/j.bandc.2016.08.009.

PILLAR TWO
Day 3: Success Without Stress

1. Véronique L. Roger et al., *Heart Disease and Stroke Statistics – 2012 Update: A Report from the American*

Heart Association (Dallas: American Heart Association, 2012).

2. Robert H. Schneider, Charles N. Alexander et al., 'Long-Term Effects of Stress Reduction on Mortality in Persons ≥55 Years of Age with Systemic Hypertension,' *American Journal of Cardiology* 95, no. 9 (1 May 2005): 1060–64; Robert H. Schneider, Frank Staggers et al., 'A Randomized Controlled Trial of Stress Reduction for Hypertension in Older African Americans,' *Hypertension* 26 (1 November 1995): 820–27; C. N. Alexander et al., 'Effects of Transcendental Meditation on Psychological Risk Factors, Cardiovascular and All-Cause Mortality: A Review of Meta-Analyses and Controlled Clinical Trials,' paper presented at the Tenth Conference of the European Health Psychology Society, Dublin, Ireland, September 1996.

3. University of Kentucky, 'Transcendental Meditation Effective in Reducing High Blood Pressure, Study Shows,' last modified 5 December 2007, www.science daily.com/releases/2007/12/071204121953.htm.

4. Schneider et al., 'Long-Term Effects of Stress Reduction on Mortality,' 1060–64.

5. Robert H. Schneider et al., 'Stress Reduction in the Secondary Prevention of Cardiovascular Disease: Randomized, Controlled Trial of Transcendental Meditation and Health Education in Blacks,' *Circulation, Cardiovascular Quality and Outcomes* 5, no. 6 (November 2012): 750–58.

6. R. D. Brook et al., on behalf of the American Heart Association Professional Education Committee of the Council for High Blood Pressure Research; Council on Cardiovascular and Stroke Nursing; Council on Epidemiology and Prevention; and Council on Nutrition, Physical Activity and Metabolism, 'Beyond Medications and Diet: Alternative Approaches to Lowering Blood Pressure – A Scientific Statement from the American Heart Association,' *Hypertension* 61, no. 6 (June 2013): 1360–83.

7. Vernon A. Barnes, Frank A. Treiber, and Harry Davis, 'Impact of Transcendental Meditation® on Cardiovascular Function at Rest and During Acute Stress in Adolescents with High Normal Blood Pressure,' *Journal of Psychosomatic Research* 51, no. 4 (October 2001): 597–605, https://doi.org/10.1161/HYP.0b013e318293645.

Day 4: Growing the Benefits

8. Fred Travis et al., 'A Self-Referential Default Brain State: Patterns of Coherence, Power, and eLORETA Sources During Eyes-Closed Rest and Transcendental Meditation Practice,' *Cognitive Processing* 11, no. 1 (February 2010): 21–30, doi:10.1007/s10339-009-0343-2, Epub 28 October 2009.

9. Harald S. Harung et al., 'Higher Psycho-Physiological Refinement in World-Class Norwegian Athletes:

Brain Measures of Performance Capacity,' *Scandinavian Journal of Medicine & Science in Sports* 21, no. 1 (February 2011): 32–41, doi:10.1111/j.1600 -0838.2009.01007.x.

10. Harald S. Harung and Frederick Travis, 'Higher Mind-Brain Development in Successful Leaders: Testing a Unified Theory of Performance,' *Cognitive Processing* 13, no. 2 (May 2012): 171–81, doi:10.1007/s10339-011 -0432-x.

11. B. Rael Cahn and John Polich, 'Meditation States and Traits: EEG, ERP, and Neuroimaging Studies,' *Psychological Bulletin* 132, no. 2 (March 2006): 180–211.

PILLAR THREE
Change Begins Within

1. Leo Shane III and Patricia Kime, 'New VA Study Finds 20 Veterans Commit Suicide Each Day,' *Military Times* online, last modified 7 July 2016, www.militarytimes. com/veterans/2016/07/07/new-va-study-finds-20 -veterans-commit-suicide-each-day.

2. Terri Tanielian and Lisa H. Jaycox, eds., *Invisible Wounds of War: Psychological and Cognitive Injuries, Their Consequences, and Services to Assist Recovery* (Santa Monica, CA: Rand Center for Military Health Policy Research, 2008), www.rand.org/content/dam/rand /pubs/monographs/2008/RAND_MG720.pdf.

3. James S. Brooks and Thomas Scarano, 'Transcendental

Meditation in the Treatment of Post-Vietnam Adjustment,' *Journal of Counseling & Development* 64, no. 3 (November 1985): 212–15.

4. Joshua Z. Rosenthal et al., 'Effects of Transcendental Meditation in Veterans of Operation Enduring Freedom and Operation Iraqi Freedom with Post-Traumatic Stress Disorder: A Pilot Study,' *Military Medicine* 176, no. 6 (June 2011): 626–30.

My Own Story

5. Sanford Nidich et al., 'Academic Achievement and Transcendental Meditation: A Study with At-Risk Urban Middle School Students,' *Education* 131, no. 3 (Spring 2011): 556–64, Education Resources Information Center (ERIC).

6. Vernon A. Barnes, Lynnette B. Bauza, and Frank L. Trieber, 'Impact of Stress Reduction on Negative School Behavior in Adolescents,' *Health and Quality of Life Outcomes* 1, no. 1 (December 2003): article 10, doi:10.1186/1477-7525-1-10.

7. Charles Elder et al., 'Effect of Transcendental Meditation on Employee Stress, Depression, and Burnout: A Randomized Controlled Study,' *Permanente Journal* 18, no. 1 (Winter 2014): 19–23, doi:10.7812/TPP /13-102.

David Lynch Foundation UK
Enquiries:
Tel: 0044 (0)845 605 8660
info@DavidLynchFoundation.org.uk
DavidLynchFoundation.org.uk

UK TM Centres

UK National TM
UK.tm.org
Tel.: 0044 1695 51213

England

London/Canary Warf	uk.tm.org/london-canary-wharf
London/City and East	uk.tm.org/london-city-and-east
London/Harrow	uk.tm.org/london-harrow
London/North West	uk.tm.org/london-north-west
London/Shepherds Bush	uk.tm.org/london-shepherds-bush
London/South	uk.tm.org/london-south-bromley
London/Twickenham	uk.tm.org/twickenham
London/Victoria	uk.tm.org/london-victoria
Birmingham	uk.tm.org/web/birmingham
Bolton	uk.tm.org/bolton
Bournemouth	uk.tm.org/bournemouth
Brighton	uk.tm.org/brighton

Bristol	uk.tm.org/bristol
Cambridge	uk.tm.org/cambridge
Chilterns	uk.tm.org/chilterns
Colchester/Essex	uk.tm.org/essex
Cornwall/Devon	uk.tm.org/devon
Essex	uk.tm.org/south-essex
Hampshire	uk.tm.org/hampshire
Lancashire	uk.tm.org/skelmersdale
Leeds	uk.tm.org/west-yorkshire
Liverpool	uk.tm.org/liverpool
Manchester	uk.tm.org/manchester
Nottingham	uk.tm.org/nottingham
Oxford	uk.tm.org/oxford

Scotland

Aberdeen	uk.tm.org/aberdeen
Edinburgh	uk.tm.org/edinburgh
Glasgow	uk.tm.org/glasgow

Wales

Cardiff/South Wales	uk.tm.org/web/cardiff-south-wales
North Wales	uk.tm.org/north-wales

Northern Ireland

Belfast	tmnorthernireland.org

Australia TM Centres

Australia National TM

tm.org.au
Tel.: 1300-886-397

Australian Capital Territory

Canberra	tm.org.au/canberra

New South Wales

Albury/Wodonga	tm.org.au/transcendental-meditation-albury-wodonga
Dubbo	tm.org.au/dubbo
Merimbula	tm.org.au/merimbula
Newcastle/Central Coast	tm.org.au/newcastle
Sydney	tm.org.au/sydney
Sydney – Mosman	tm.org.au/mosman-tm-for-women
Sydney – Summer Hill	tm.org.au/summer-hill-tm-for-women
Wollongong	tm.org.au/wollongong

Northern Territory

Darwin	tm.org.au/darwin

Queensland

Brisbane	tm.org.au/brisbane
Cairns	tm.org.au/cairns
Gold Coast	tm.org.au/gold-coast
Noosa	tm.org.au/noosa
Sunshine Coast	tm.org.au/sunshine-coast
Toowoomba	tm.org.au/toowoomba

South Australia

Adelaide	tm.org.au/adelaide
Adelaide South	tm.org.au/transcendental-meditation-adelaide-south

Victoria

Bundoora	tm.org.au/bundoora
Geelong	tm.org.au/geelong
Hastings	tm.org.au/hastings
Mansfield	tm.org.au/mansfield
Melbourne – Mentone	tm.org.au/mentone

Melbourne – Mornington   tm.org.au/mornington
Melbourne – Mount Eliza   tm.org.au/mount-eliza
Melbourne – North   tm.org.au/melbourne-reservoir
Melbourne – Ringwood   tm.org.au/ringwood
Melbourne - St Kilda Road   tm.org.au/melbourne-stkilda

Western Australia
Busselton   tm.org.au/busselton

New Zealand TM Centres

New Zealand National TM
tm.org.nz
Tel.: 0800 212 345

TM centres

Auckland Mount Wellington   tm.org.nz/auckland-mtwellington
Auckland North Shore   tm.org.nz/auckland-north-shore
Auckland Ponsonby   tm.org.nz/auckland-ponsonby
Christchurch Central   tm.org.nz/christchurch-central
Christchurch West   tm.org.nz/christchurch-west
Hawkes Bay   tm.org.nz/hawkes-bay
KatiKati   tm.org.nz/katikati
Nelson   tm.org.nz/nelson
Northland   tm.org.nz/northland
Opotiki and Eastern   tm.org.nz/opotiki
Bay of Plenty
Palmerston North   tm.org.nz/palmerston-north
Rotorua   tm.org.nz/rotorua
Tauranga   tm.org.nz/tauranga
Wellington   tm.org.nz/wellington
Western Bay of Plenty   tm.org.nz/western-bay-of-plenty-
Tanners Point   tanners-point

ABOUT THE AUTHOR

BOB ROTH is one the most experienced and sought-after meditation teachers in America. Over the past forty-five years, Bob has taught Transcendental Meditation to thousands of people. He currently serves as the CEO of the David Lynch Foundation and also directs the Center for Leadership Performance in New York. Bob is the host of the SiriusXM radio show *Success Without Stress* and has spoken about meditation to industry leaders at gatherings such as Google Zeitgeist, Aspen Ideas Festival, Wisdom 2.0 and Summit.